Contents

Music Theory for Fretboarders

Jared E. Davis

The fretboard is one of the most confusing and difficult landscapes to navigate. It is nothing like the visually symmetrical layout of a piano. What makes it even more difficult than just the impossible layout of the fretboard, is that most guitarists are learning from tablature. Don't get me wrong, tablature is a great communication tool. It can tell you exactly which fret and string to put your fingers on, but it leaves out some very crucial information. It doesn't show you the notes or the music theory behind them. I am here to fill in those gaps.

In this lecture you will learn 3 things.

1. Basic Music Theory
2. All the notes on the fretboard
3. How to put them together visually

I have learned some amazing shortcuts for my students over the last few years and I am excited to share them all with you. I will give you all the information I wish someone gave me when I first picked up a guitar. I was a self-taught guitarist and learned exclusively from tablature for years. I never knew the notes and I definitely did not know any music theory. I would mostly play by ear if there wasn't tablature around and I would really struggle to find the right notes and scales that went with a song. It wasn't until I attended music school that I began to learn these skills, and as a "self-taught tablature guitarist" (STTG for short) it was very difficult to keep up with everyone else. However, being an STTG is exactly the reason why I was able to find these shortcuts to finally make sense of the fretboard. So, without any more introductions, let's jump right in!

Lesson 1: Single String Theory

Before we start learning to memorize and read notes, we have to learn some theory. In music we only have 12 notes. This is true no matter what instrument you play. The piano, flute, violin, and guitar all use the same 12 notes. The easiest way to understand this on your fretboard is to count on one string from fret 0 to fret 11. (0 is the open string)

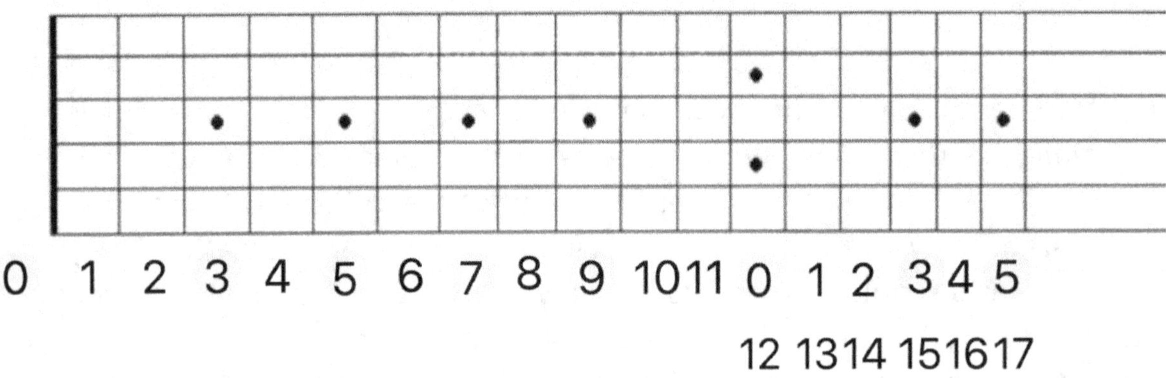

You'll notice at the 12th fret there are usually 2 dots that mark the fret. All the fret dots are there to help you count frets, but those 2 dots are there to tell you that the notes of each string are starting over from 0 again. The note on the 12th fret is the same note as the open string note 0. Try it on all 6 strings. You can also test this by playing 0 1 then skip to 12 13 to hear how the notes sound the same. This is a term we call an "Octave". 12 and 13 are the same note as 0 and 1, but the pitch sounds twice as high. You can use this term octave to say 12 and 13 are an octave higher than 0 and 1 or 0 and 1 are an octave lower than 12 and 13.

Since there are only 12 notes, that means the distance between any 2 notes can only be 11 or less. We call the distance between 2 notes an "Interval". That interval you heard when you played 0 to 1 or 12 to 13 is called a "Semi-Tone" or "Half-Step". Each fret represents a half-step no matter where you are. When you counted from 0 to 12 you were counting by half-steps. When you play all 12 notes by half-steps, it is called the "Chromatic" scale. The 12-note chromatic scale divides the distance of an octave into 12 equal parts. 12 half-steps, 12 notes.

Intervals

The next interval is a "Whole-Step" or "Tone". This is the distance of two half-steps or two frets. If you play whole-steps on a single string 0 2 4 6 8 10 12, this is called the "Whole-Tone" scale. It divides the distance of an octave into 6 equal parts. 6 whole steps that again, will repeat from the beginning at the 12th fret.

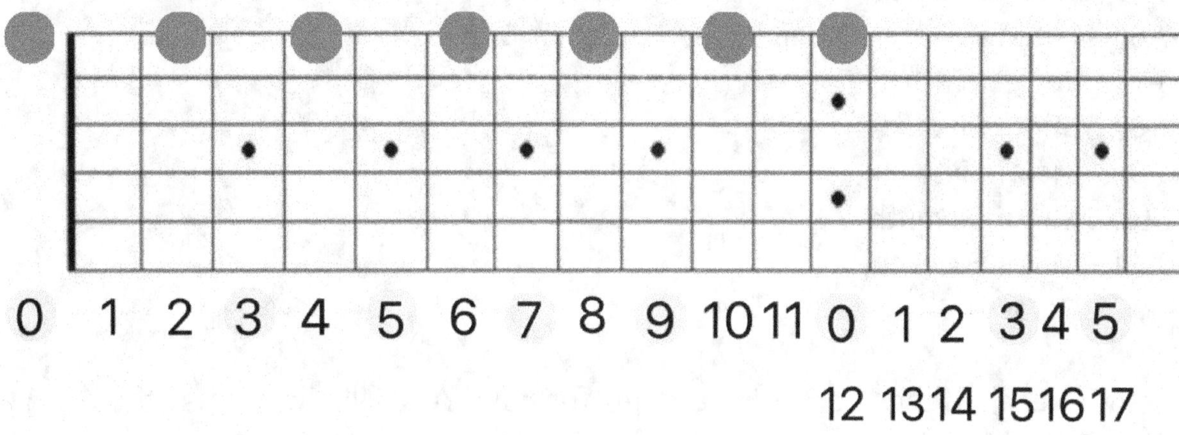

As a friendly warning, I will say there are lots of terms we have to memorize, but the good news is that most of music theory is really just knowing the terms. The terms communicate what is happening in the music and it's what we all use when we communicate with other musicians.

So far, we have learned,

3 intervals - Octave, Half-Step, Whole-Step,
2 scales - Chromatic scale, Whole-Tone scale.

I won't go over every single interval in detail just yet, but you should start to memorize how many half-steps each interval is made of and what each interval sounds like. We use interval names (seconds-sevenths) because they are derived from the seven-note "major" scale. I will explain more on that later.

Here is a list of all the intervals from the 12-note chromatic scale. Because they are derived from the chromatic scale, we call them "Chromatic Intervals".

0-0   Unison
0-1   Minor Second   (Half-Step)
0-2   Major Second   (Whole-Step)
0-3   Minor Third
0-4   Major Third
0-5   Perfect Fourth
0-6   Tritone   (Augmented Fourth or Diminished Fifth)
0-7   Perfect Fifth
0-8   Minor Sixth
0-9   Major Sixth
0-10 Minor Seventh
0-11 Major seventh
0-12 Octave

Practice each of these on a single string for now. You will always play the open 0 first, then the next fret number to hear the interval. Saying the interval names out loud when you play them will help your brain to remember. The interval numbers will always match the fret number.

The Major Scale

You most likely have heard of the "Major" scale before. If you have ever been in a children's music class (it's the one thing you were forced to sing), or if you have ever seen "The Sound of Music", you should know - Do Re Mi Fa So La Ti Do.

The major scale is the most important tool to learn when it comes to western music. It is a 7-note combination of whole-steps and half-steps and it is very helpful to visualize it on one string. The pattern is WWHWWWH. W=Whole-Step and H=Half-Step. You should practice thinking about the major scale in 3 ways,

1. The pattern WWHWWWH
2. Do Re Mi Fa So La Ti Do   (This technique is called "Solfège")
3. Scale degrees 1234567

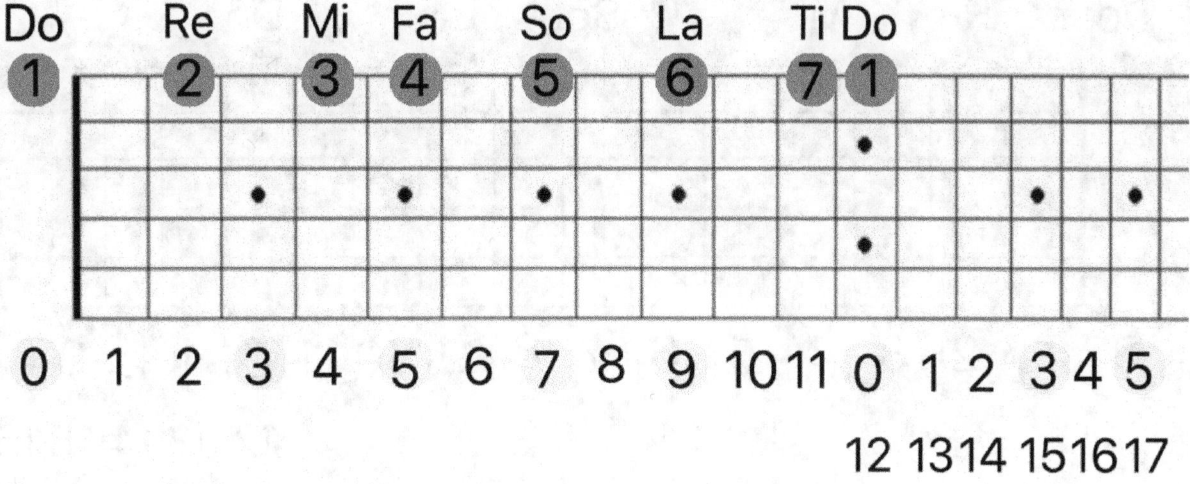

You can practice this on each string. Say the pattern and scale degrees out loud as you play, sing the solfege as you play. Remember it will start over from the beginning at the 12th fret. You should also do it backwards starting from the 12th fret. Don't be shy to sing. Trust me when I say that singing is one of the most powerful tools for training our ears and brain. An important thing to note is that there are only two half-step intervals between 3-4 (Mi-Fa) and 7-1 (Ti-Do). All the other intervals are whole-steps.

Things we derive from the Major scale

As I said before, the major scale is one of the main foundations of music and there are some important things we can take from it. As a guitarist I'm sure you know the term "Pentatonic". A pentatonic scale is made from taking a 7-note scale and turning it into a 5-note scale (Penta means 5). All we have to do is take away 2 notes. The major scale pentatonic is made by subtracting the 4th and 7th scale degrees. Giving us only 1 2 3 5 6 or Do Re Mi So La.

This skipping of notes is called "Leaping". Moving from one note to the next closest is called "Stepping". Hence the previous terms, half-step and whole-step. Unlike the major scale, which is only made of steps, the pentatonic scale is interesting because it contains steps and leaps.

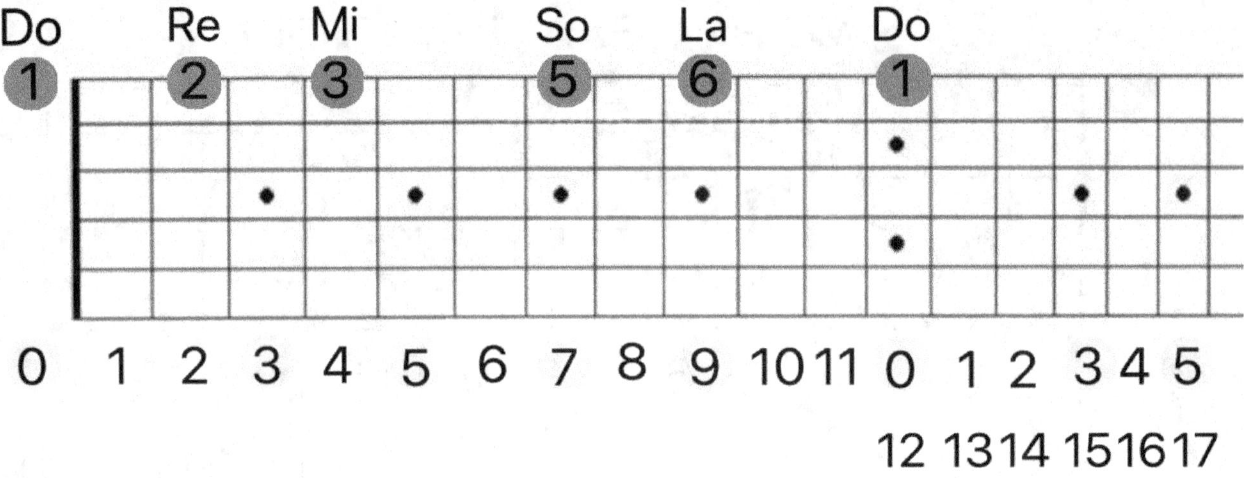

Can you see the pattern? Step step leap step leap. Leaping is a useful term. We can make many different kinds of leaps inside the major scale. Moving from 1-2 or 2-3 would be called a step or moving by "Seconds". If we move from 1-3 or 2-4 or 3-5 etc., this is called a leap of a "Third". You can make a leap of a third by simply skipping over one note in the scale as we did here.

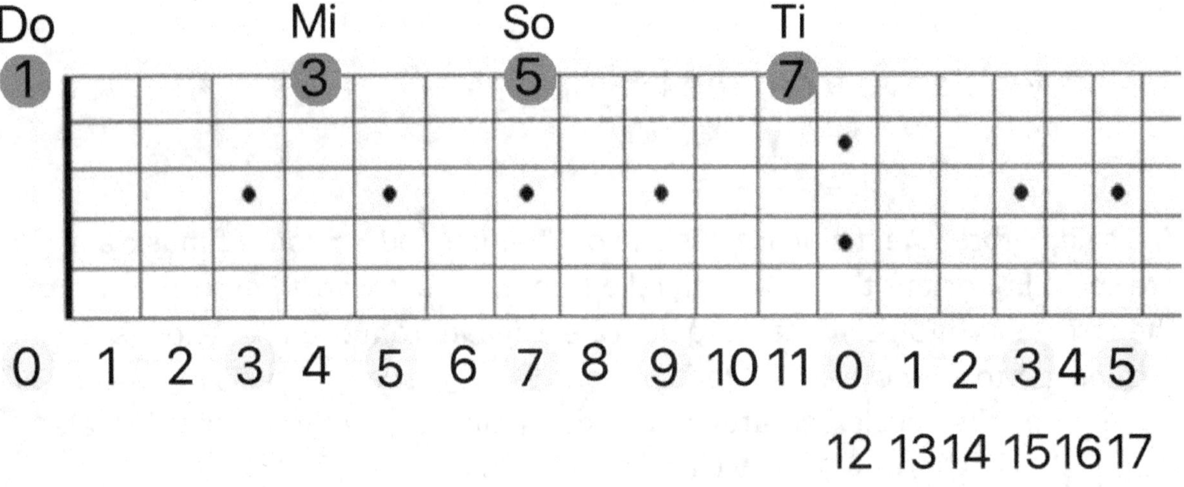

This is an example of leaping by thirds. We skip every other note in the scale. You can make other kinds of larger leaps by skipping more than one note. Here is a list of steps and leaps within a major scale.

Seconds   = steps, no skipping
Thirds   = skipping over one note
Fourths   = skipping over two notes
Fifths   = skipping over three notes
Sixth   = skipping over four notes
Sevenths = skipping over five notes

The easiest way to remember this is to always start from the 1st scale degree.

1-2 = second
1-3 = third
1-4 = fourth
1-5 = fifth
1-6 = sixth
1-7 = seventh

We call these steps and leaps "Diatonic Intervals". "Diatonic" is a term that means we are limited to only steps and leaps within the major scale. Since they are diatonic, we don't have to be as specific as the chromatic interval names. We just say second, third, fourth, etc.

Chords

We can also create "chords" from the major scale. Typically, a chord is a stack of 3 or more notes. A stack of 3 notes is called a "Triad". We can make a triad from each of the seven scale degrees by stacking notes in thirds. For example:

135   Do Mi So
246   Re Fa La
357   Mi So Ti
461   Fa La Do
572   So Ti Re
613   La Do Mi
724   Ti Re Fa

These are called "Diatonic Chords" or "Diatonic Triads". More on this later.

Lesson 1 Review

There are 12 notes in music that we call the chromatic scale. The chromatic scale is divided into 12 equal parts called half-steps. You can see this on your fretboard because each fret represents a half-step. You can also see where the chromatic scale starts over at the next octave because it is marked by 2 dots at the 12th fret.

There are 12 possible intervals. We call them chromatic intervals because they come from the chromatic scale.

Two half-steps make a whole-step. The octave can be divided into 6 equal whole-steps. We call that scale the whole-tone scale.

The major scale (Do-Re-Mi-Fa-So-La-Ti) is a 7-note pattern of half and whole-steps (WWHWWWH). When you limit yourself to only the notes of the major scale, these notes are called diatonic. We can make many things from diatonic notes, such as diatonic intervals of seconds through sevenths.

We can also make a pentatonic scale (5-note scale) by removing the 4th and 7th scale degrees. Giving us only Do-Re-Mi-So-La or scale degrees 1-2-3-5-6.

Diatonic chords can be made from each of the seven scale degrees. We can make 3-note chords called triads by stacking 3 notes in thirds. We call these diatonic triads.

Remember diatonic means to only use notes, intervals, scales and chords from the major scale. If you use any other notes outside of the major scale, you must call it chromatic because it comes from the chromatic scale.

Lesson 2: The Notes

Now that I have thrown a bunch of theory at you, it's time to talk about the actual note names. Even though there are 12 notes in music, we only use 7 letter names A-B-C-D-E-F-G. This is because western music notation was so heavily based on the 7-note major scale, the C major scale to be more precise. In fact, the piano is the best example because it was built around the C major scale.

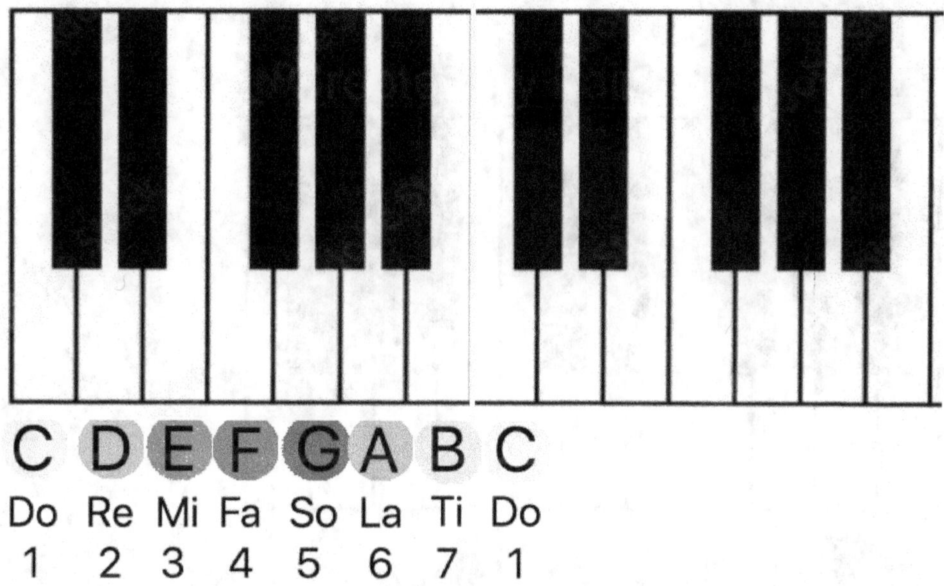

Each key of the piano represents a half-step, just like the frets on your guitar. However, the piano is visually representing a major scale. The white keys of the piano are visually showing us the WWHWWWH pattern for a major scale. The major scale pattern starts on the note C, and repeats at the next octave C.

Can you see that the black keys are the notes we skip over to make the major scale pattern? If you count every key from C to the next C, you get a total of 12 keys. These 12 keys represent the same 12 notes we use on the guitar frets. This time instead of skipping over a fret, the black keys are the notes we skip over.

Notice between B-C and E-F there is no black key. This is important to remember.

All of this is extremely important because the C major scale is the parent scale of all music. It represents the letter names of all the notes without adding any sharps or flats. What are sharps and flats?

Well, since we only have 7 letter names, we needed a way of naming all the other notes. Sharps and flats are called "accidentals".

A sharp, which looks like this pound sign #, means to go up one half-step.

A flat, which looks like a crooked lower-case *b,* means to go down one half-step.

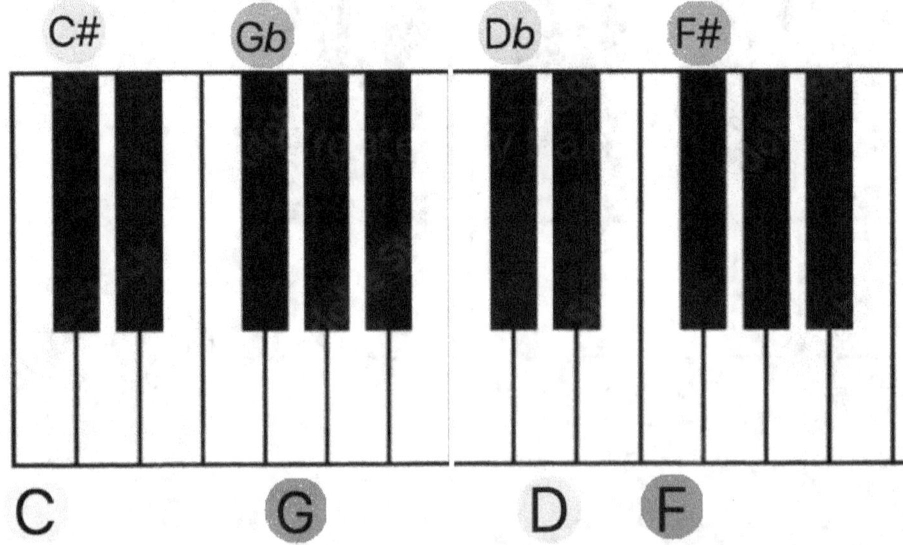

C# is one key higher than C, so we have to play the black key right above it.

G*b* is one key lower than G, so we have to play the black key right below it.

Now I have to point out a term called "Enharmonic". Enharmonic notes are two different letter spellings that represent the same note.

For example, if I say play D*b*, you would play the black key lower than D, but that is the same key as C#. Same scenario for G*b*/F#. Every black key has 2 names.

There is a reason for this, but don't worry too much about it now. Just remember sharp # is up, flat *b* is down, and every black key has 2 names. A sharp and flat.

Fretboard Notes

You are probably already aware of the way we tune the strings, EADGBE. These are not just the string names; they are the actual note names of the open string notes or fret 0 notes.

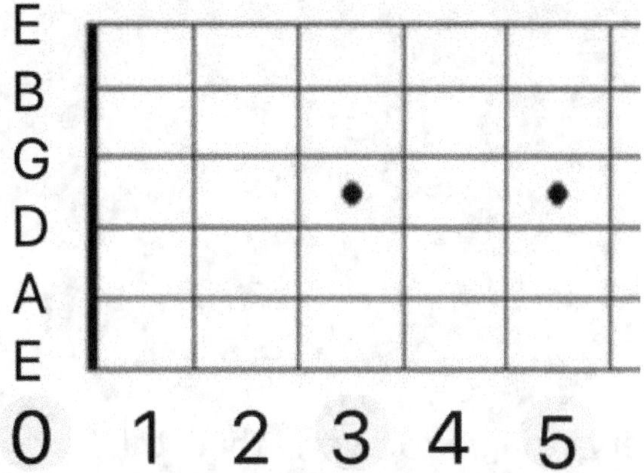

If you wanted to start naming the notes of each fret on each string, you could just start counting up the fret numbers from each of those starting notes. When you do this, you have to remember which notes are missing a black key in between them. B-C and E-F do not have a black key between them, which means there is no sharp or flat note between them. They will be right next to each other.

On the E strings, the first fret note is F, and the first fret note on the B string is C.

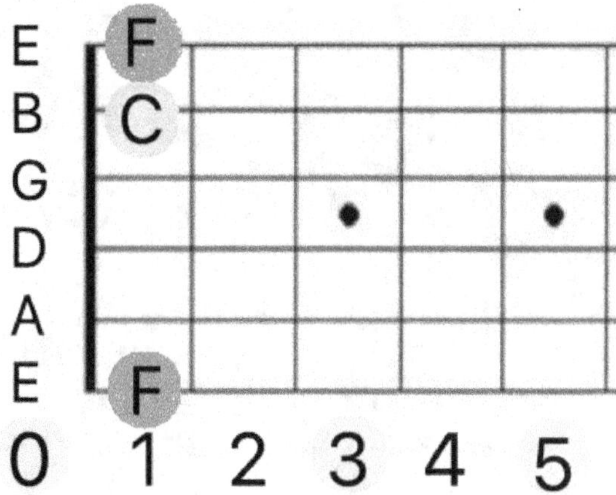

All other notes have a black key in between them, so they will have a sharp or flat between them. You can start by only using sharps first, then do flats after. In jazz we typically use sharps going up and flats going down.

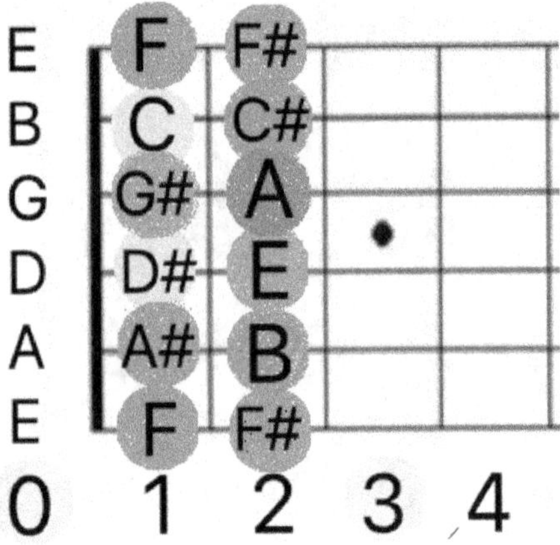

You could do this for every position and every string; however, I think this is a horrible way to memorize the notes on the fretboard. We as humans need to see a visual pattern, not count every single fret in a row and try to mindlessly memorize what the order of notes is.

The best way to start memorizing the notes on the fretboard is to learn the C major scale in each position and on each string. We have to think like a piano player! If we've already memorized the notes that have no sharps or flats, then all we have to do is go up or down 1 fret to find the flat or sharp note.

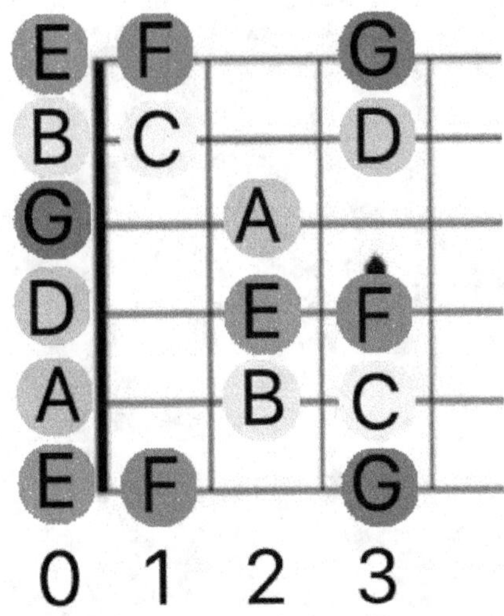

Start with this open position. Remember C is Do.

You can also start memorizing the C major scale horizontally on just the A string.
C to C is our 7-note major scale WWHWWWH pattern - Do Re Mi Fa So La Ti Do.

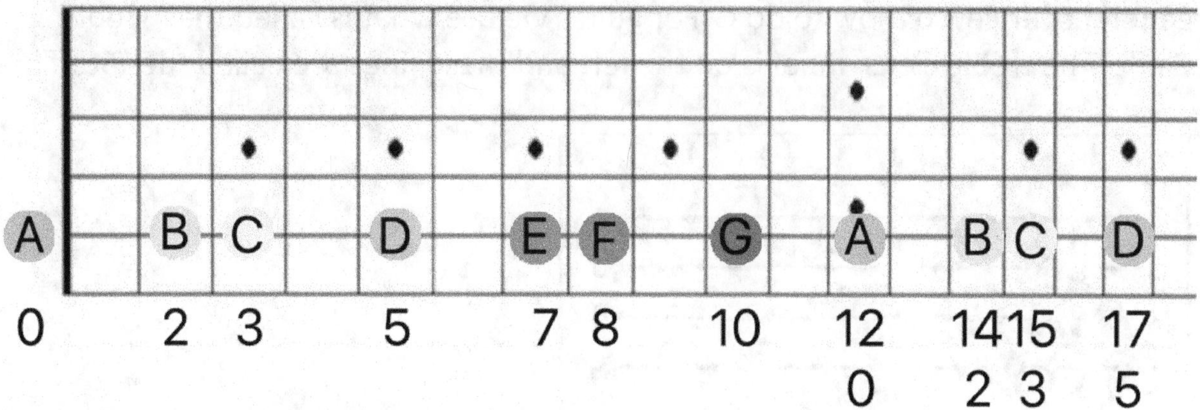

You can make flashcards of A-G to test your knowledge of the C major notes.
Make sure to identify every note the flashcard gives you. For example, if you drew
B, 2 different frets have B. Therefore, you would need to identify both.

Practice the open position and the A string as separate exercises. Once mastered,
you can make 12 flashcards of all 12 notes with sharps and flats.

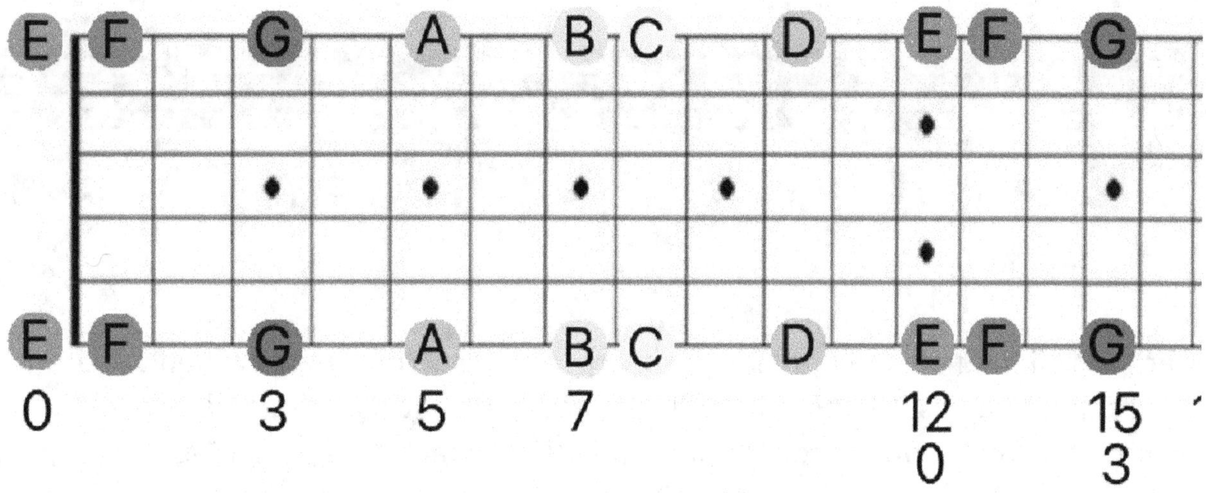

The guitar has 2 E-strings, so memorizing them will kill two birds with one stone.
The E and A strings are the most important strings to memorize because most of
our chords and scales are built from them. Burn them into your brain!

Reading Music

This book is not about sight reading music notation, but I want to give you a general overview of how to do it. For guitar we use what is called the "Treble Clef". The treble clef symbol is on the left and these lines are called the "Staff".

Each line and each space represent notes of the C major scale. The most typical way students are taught to remember the lines is "Every Good Boy Does Fine", and for the spaces they spell "FACE". The spaces are thirds away from each other, so we skip over a letter when counting by space. Same thing for counting by lines.

Here are all the notes of C major (no sharps or flats). You can see when we count by seconds like this, that we count line-space-line-space. As I said before, counting by thirds would be skipping over a letter each time, meaning you would be counting by spaces or lines only. Space-space-space or line-line-line.

We also have notes above and below the staff. The lines that extend beyond the staff lines are called "ledger lines". It is very normal to read notes from ledger lines.

Adding accidentals (sharps and flats) to notes.

The notes work the same way on paper as they do on the instruments. If you add a sharp to the note, you move it up by one half-step, and down by one half-step for flats.

We do still have to maintain the rule about enharmonic notes. So, A# and Bb are the same note, and so are Eb and D#. This will make sense later on, don't worry. These are the open strings notes. The lowest E string is 3 ledger lines below.

Notes go from low to high visually and in the way they sound. Just like on guitar. You have to make sure to play the right note in the right octave. So that low E note 3 ledger lines down, can only be played with the low open E string.

The higher E note however, can be played on more than one string.

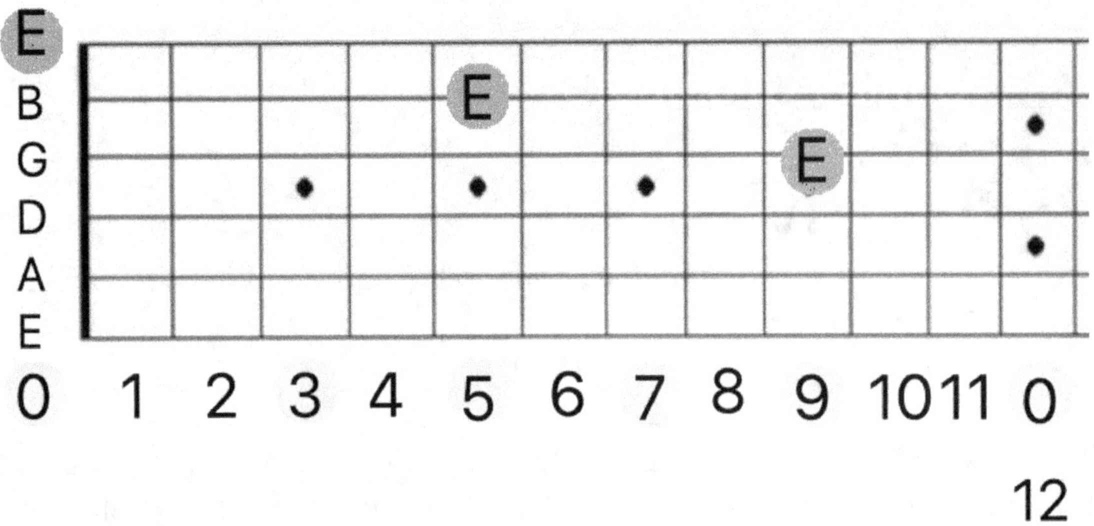

Believe it or not, but if you have 24 frets, you can play this E note on all 6 strings!

This is the reason tablature was invented. We needed to know what fret and what string to put our fingers on. Unlike piano, where there is only one key for each note, we have multiple options to play the same note.

Lesson 2 Review

There are 12 notes, but only 7 letter names A-B-C-D-E-F-G. This is because western music was based around the 7-note major scale. The C major scale.

The piano was built around the C major scale. Because the C major scale is how we count letter names without sharps or flats, the piano was made to have white keys represent those letter names.

The black keys represent sharps and flats. A sharp # is one half-step higher and a flat *b* is one half-step lower. Remember we call sharps and flats "Accidentals".

Adding accidentals (sharps and flats) to a letter, moves it by one half-step. Typically, we use sharps when going up and flats when going down.

Every black key has two note names. For example, C# is the same note as D*b*.

We call those notes "enharmonic".

All 12 notes ascending by half-step using sharps.

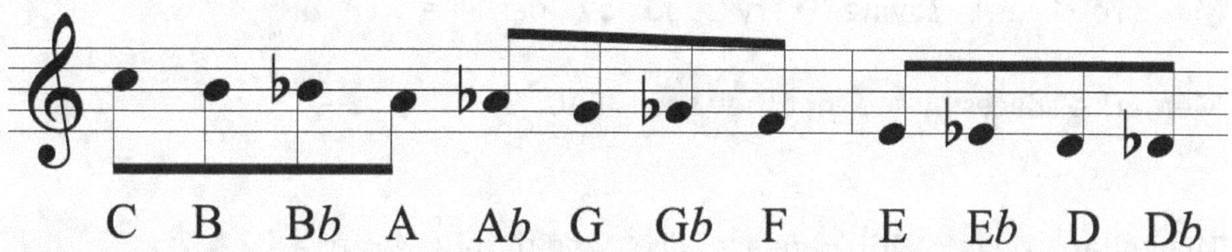

All 12 notes descending by half-steps using flats.

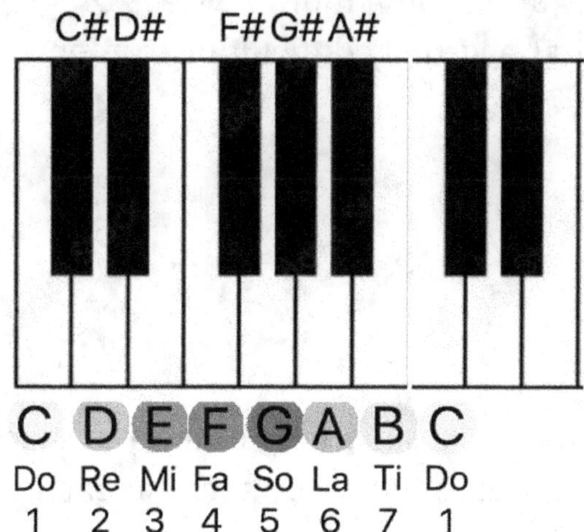

The best way to memorize the notes of the fretboard is not to count every single fret, but to memorize the C major scale. (Notes without sharps or flats)

It is very important to remember that there is no black key between B-C and E-F. This applies to your fretboard too. B-C and E-F will always be one fret away.

Once you know all the notes of the C major scale, all you have to do is move up or down by one fret to find the sharp or flat notes.

When reading music, the guitar uses the treble clef. The 5 lines are called staff lines. Lines above the staff lines are called ledger lines.

Each line and space represent note names. Going by lines only is moving in thirds, same with moving by spaces only.

Memorize lines by saying "Every Good Boy Does Fine".

Memorize spaces by see that they spell "FACE".

The guitar strings EADGBE are actually tuned to those notes.

There are multiple ways to play the same notes on different frets and strings.

The guitar having each string tuned differently and having multiple ways of playing the same notes is what makes the guitar a visually difficult instrument.

Lesson 3: String Crossings

The way we tune the 6 strings of a guitar is what makes learning notes and theory so difficult. Understanding that frets go by half-step is easy, but because each string starts with a different note, we don't get a visual symmetry like the piano.

Most of the strings are tuned 5 half-steps away from each other, the only exception is the B string. It is tuned 4 half-steps away from the G string.

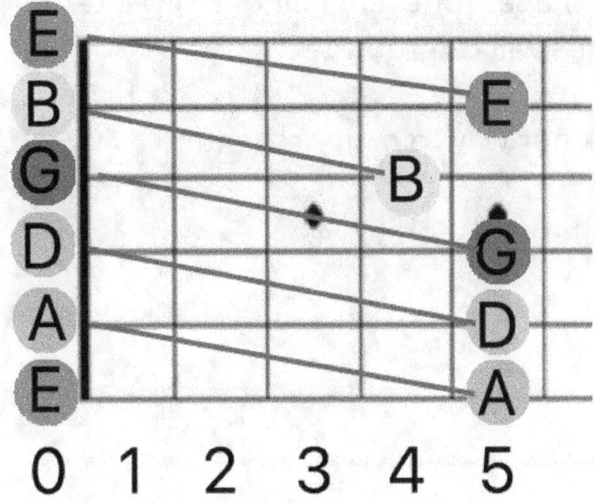

Notes on right are same as open strings. You can call these Unison notes.

Lots of players use this technique to tune their guitar without a tuner. You just match the notes of each string. So, to tune the A string, you play 5th fret E and match it to that note. You can do this for every note of the open strings on the left, and match it to the fretted notes on the right. (Except the low E string)

5 half-steps = Perfect 4th, and 4 half-steps = major 3rd. So, every string is tuned by a perfect 4th, except for the B string, which is tuned by a major 3rd.

I know it is super confusing right? And the B string? Whose idea was that anyway?

This tuning was chosen simply out of comfort for chord shapes, but don't worry, we will learn to conquer these complexities and visualize the tuning.

Double String Theory

I first showed you the 11 intervals on one single string. That was to show you how to see the number of half-steps each interval contains. Now we have to learn to do that same thing when crossing over to the next string. Intervals on 2 strings.

There are only 5 pairs of adjacent strings: E-A A-D D-G *G-B* B-E

Luckily, except for G-B, it will be the same shapes for every pair of strings. Let's call G-B group 2 and all the other string pairs will be group 1.

We will start with minor seconds and work our way to major seventh.

If you need to, you can refer back to the interval list on pg. 4.

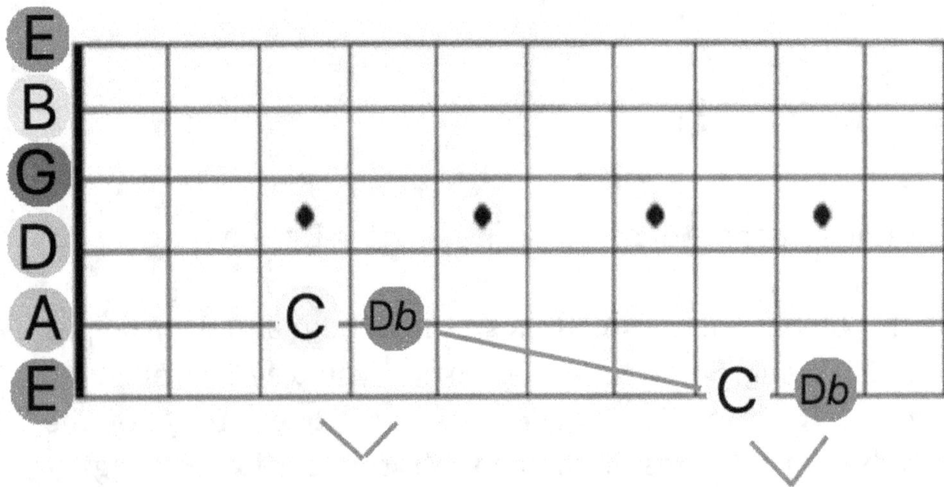

C to Db is a half-step or 1 fret away. You can clearly see that on a single string, but it's a little trickier to see it when you cross strings. This is how we make a minor second for group 1. It will always be 4 frets behind.

You play C on the E string and then Db on the A string. It will sound the same as if you played both on one string. Check note names to make sure you have it right. Here are the shapes for a minor second between 2 strings. 1 half-step.

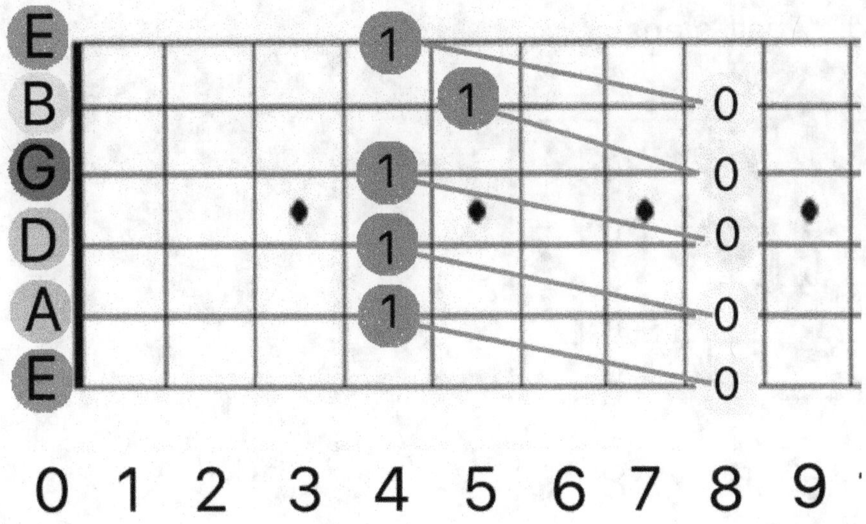

I labeled it 0-1 to show you the starting note is 0, and on the next string, the next note 1 is a half-step away. Just like how we did it on a single string from fret 0-1.

Can you see how group 2 (G-B) is the only different shape?

G-B is a major third, it's the only string pair that is not tuned by a perfect fourth. So, every interval shape will be one fret higher in group 2.

This is how you can play all 12 notes by half-step across all strings. Notice the half-step shapes when we cross strings. Only from the G to B-string is it different.

Here are diagrams of all the interval shapes in order, starting from major second.

Major second - 2 half-steps

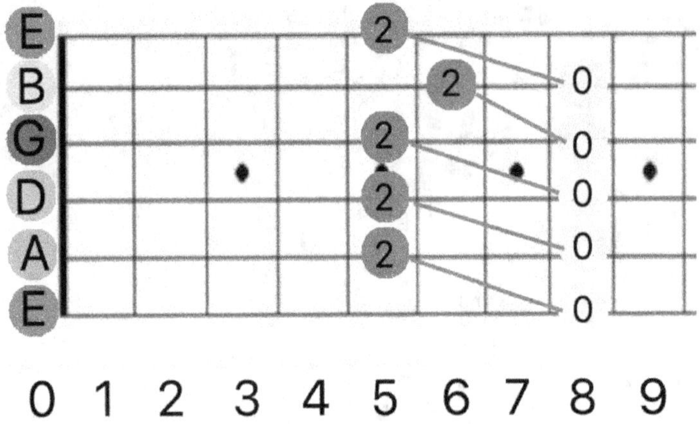

Minor third - 3 half-steps

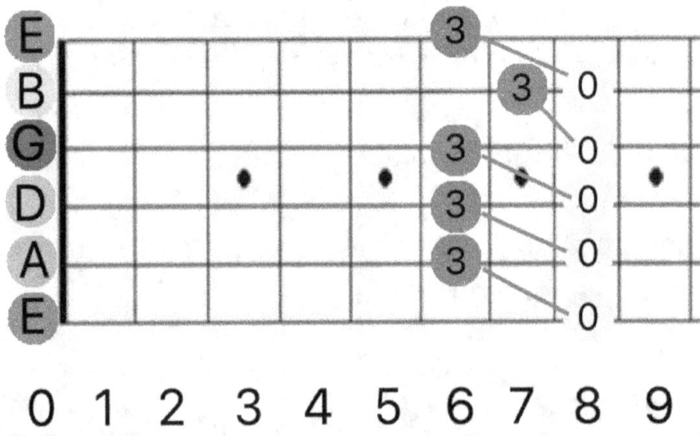

Major third - 4 half-steps

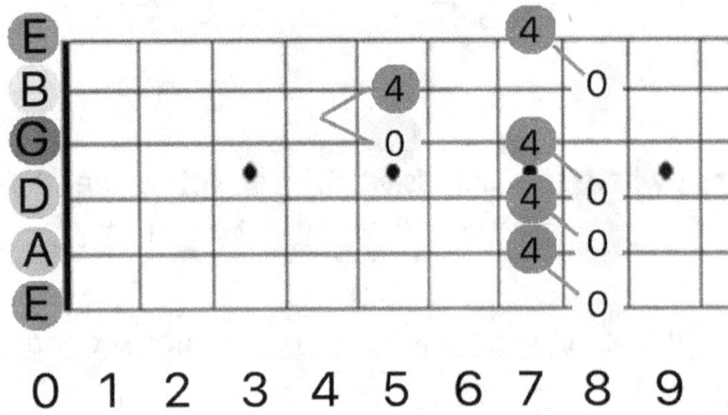

Perfect fourth - 5 half-steps

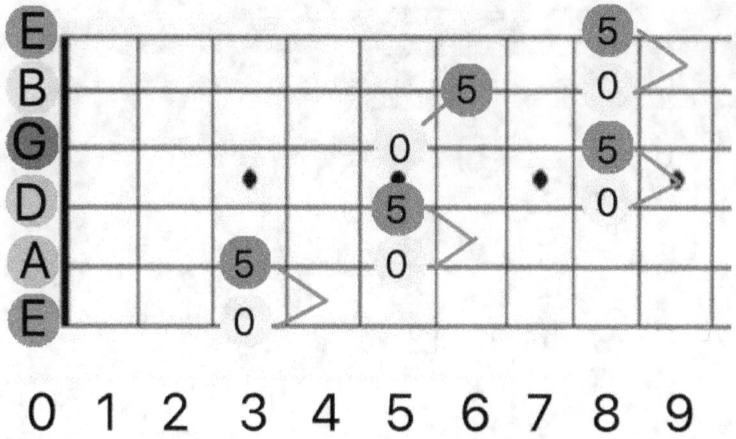

Tritone - 6 half-steps

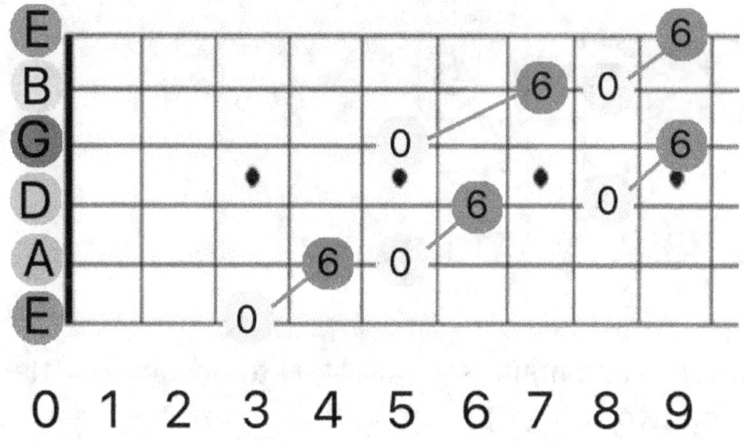

Perfect fifth - 7 half-steps

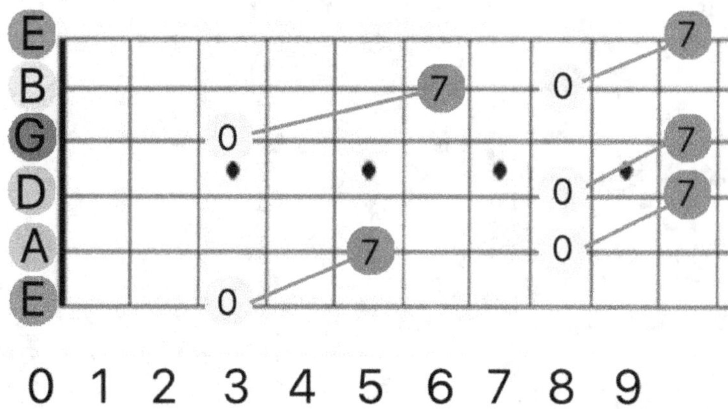

"Power Chord"

Minor sixth - 8 half-steps

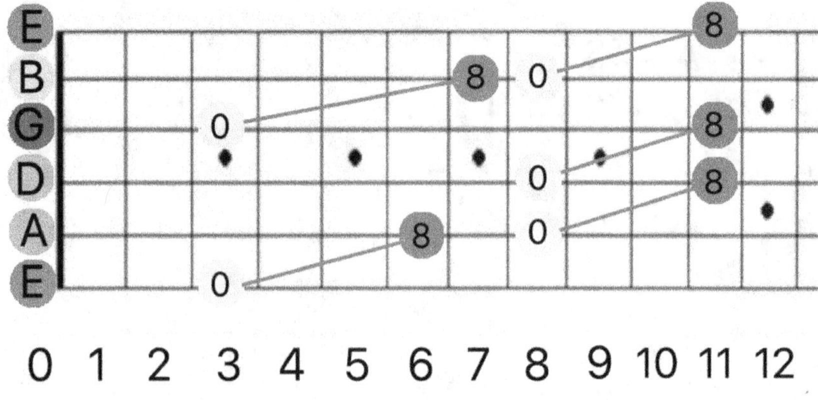

Major sixth - 9 half-steps

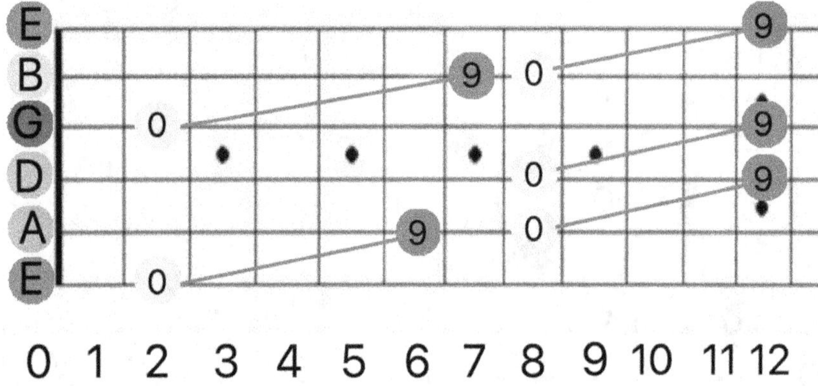

The last two intervals of minor seventh and major seventh start to become a little too big of a stretch for our hands on two strings. So, for sake of comfort, we can move the second note over to a third string. (Skip a string)

Minor seventh - 10 half-steps

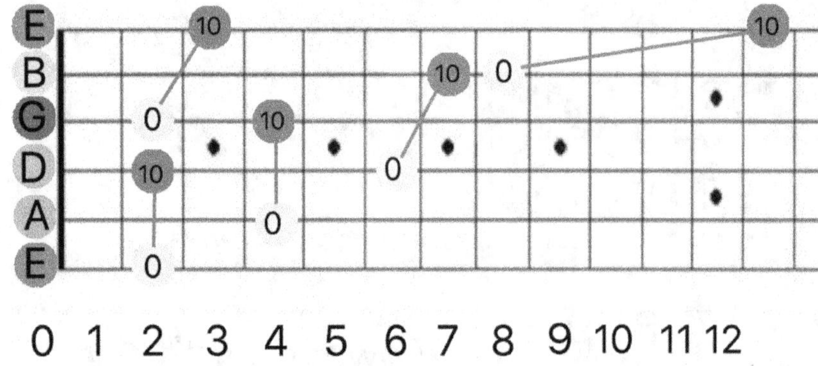

You can see how when we get to the B string, the interval gets moved up one fret again. From D-B and from G-E the interval shape gets warped by one half-step from the tuning of the B string.

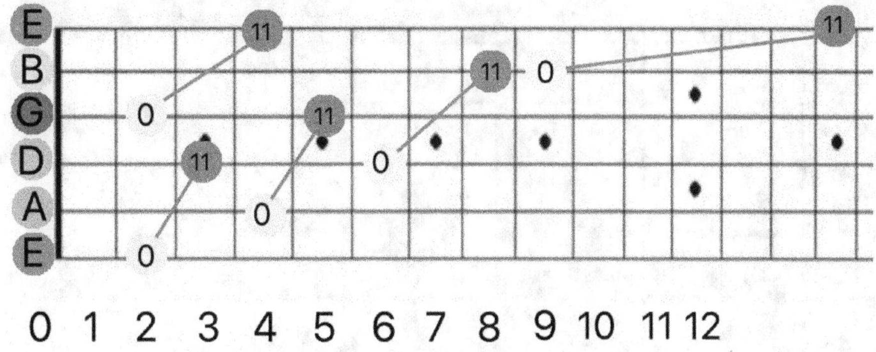

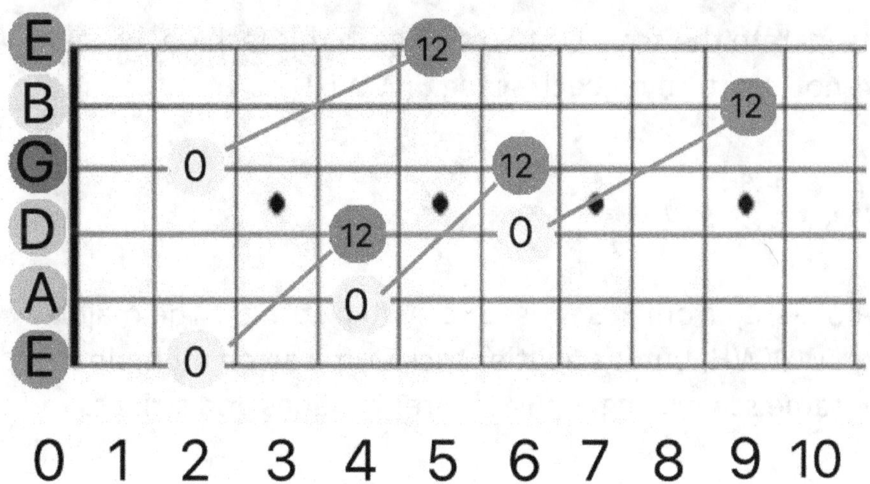

The octave shapes are great to memorize. Remember an octave is the same note, but twice as high in pitch. So, you can use it to help you memorize more notes on the fretboard. You can also use it to find major and minor seventh shapes across 3 strings, by subtracting 1-2 frets. It also sounds cool and makes a note sound fuller.

So, crossing over 1 string on the same fret adds 5 half-steps, 4 from G to B-strings. Then crossing 2 strings over on the same fret adds 10 half-steps, 9 with the B-string added in there. Starting to get it now?

Major Scale Across Strings

Now that you know the major scale pattern and can visualize it on one string, you can move to visualizing the pattern and note names on 2 strings.

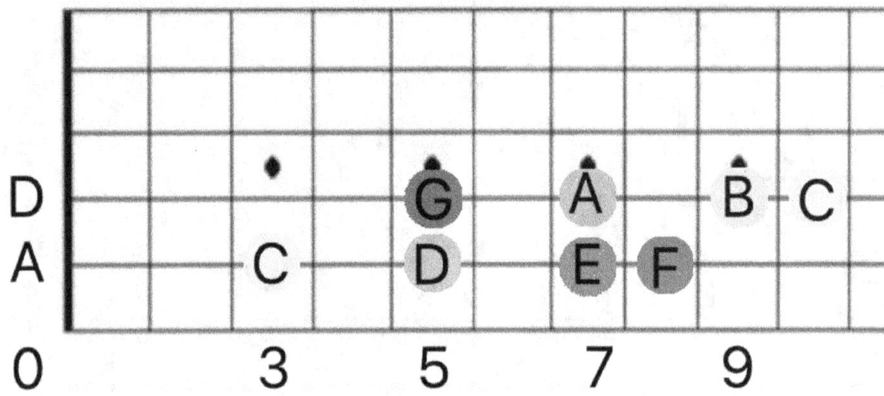

Interestingly when you separate the scale on two strings in this fashion, we get the same symmetrical 4-note pattern on each string. (WWH)

A string = Do Re Mi Fa / 1 2 3 4
D string = So La Ti Do / 5 6 7 8

Can you see how the whole-step from F-G is used to switch strings? The major scale pattern is still WWHWWWH, but it's a littler trickier to see on multiple strings. We can play the same scale using many different shapes and strings.

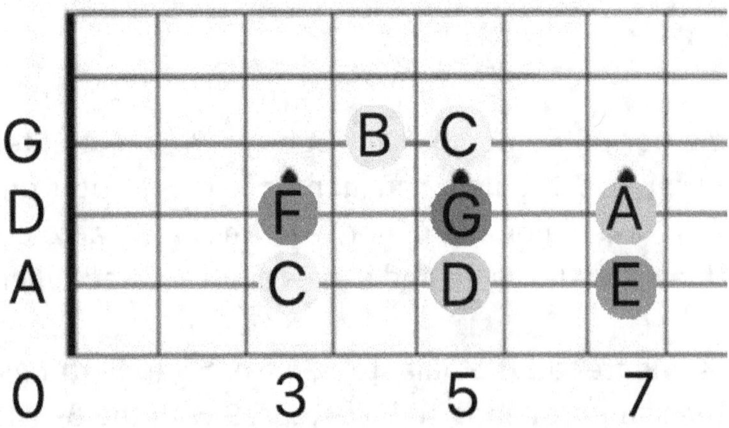

In this example we moved notes B and C to the G-string using the whole-step from A-B. This is an example of staying in one position to play a scale. Can you see how the scale fits between the octave shape from C to C?

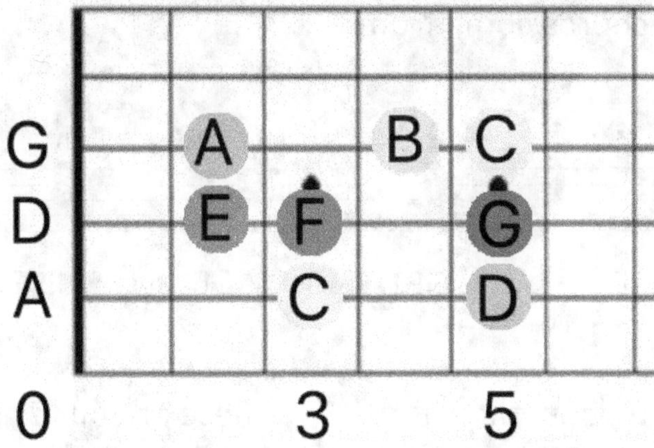

Here is another way to play the same notes and same major scale pattern across 3 strings and staying in one position. Again, we use the whole-step to cross strings. Notice the half-steps between B-C and E-F is always present.

Each of these 3 examples play the same notes in the same order. This is the burden of the guitar player. We have so many different options to play the exact same thing whereas on piano, there is only one option.

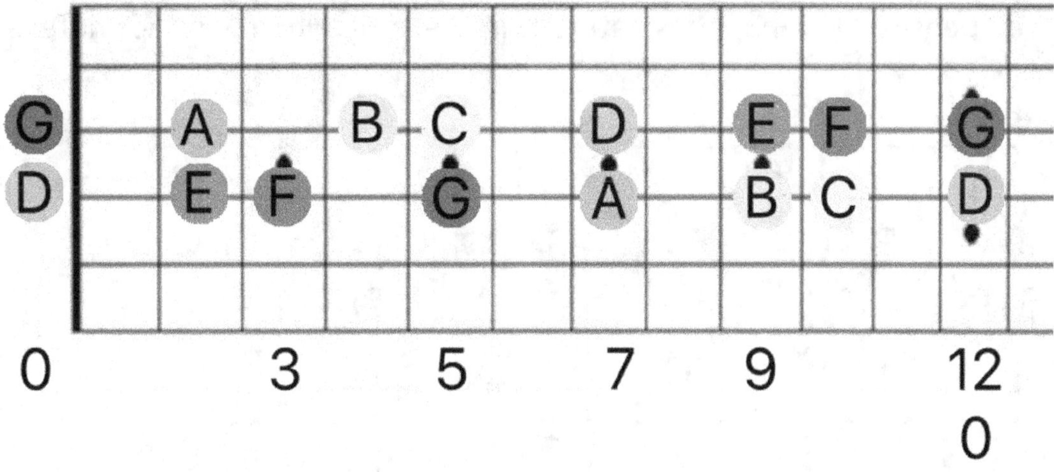

Now you can start memorizing the notes of the D and G strings.

Diatonic Chords and Modes

I briefly discussed chords in the first lesson, but now is where the details come in. Taking the notes of C major C-D-E-F-G-A-B, we will stack in thirds from each note of the scale. This is where our 7 diatonic chords come from.

In music theory we use roman numerals to label the chords 1-7. These are our 7 diatonic triads (Triad = 3-note chord). Notice how I-IV-V are upper case and ii-iii-vi are lower case. (Don't worry about vii° yet)

Upper case signifies a major triad and lower case signifies a minor triad. For lack of better words, major sounds happy and minor sounds sad.

Major chords are built by putting a minor third on top of a major third. Look at the first chord, C-E is major third (4 half-steps) and E-G is minor third (3 half-steps). The bottom note is called the "root" note. C = root.

Now look at the second chord, D-F is a minor third and F-A is a major third. See how they are opposite? This happens naturally in the scale when we stack notes.

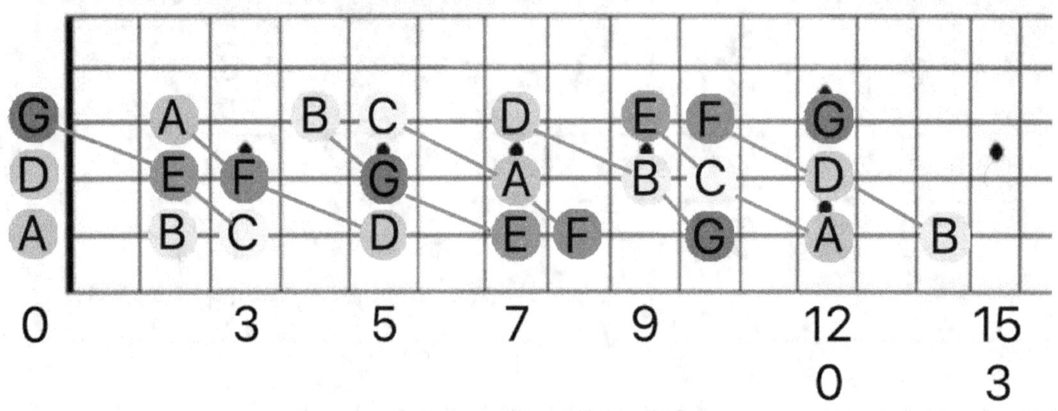

You can also visualize them in a single position with string crossings.

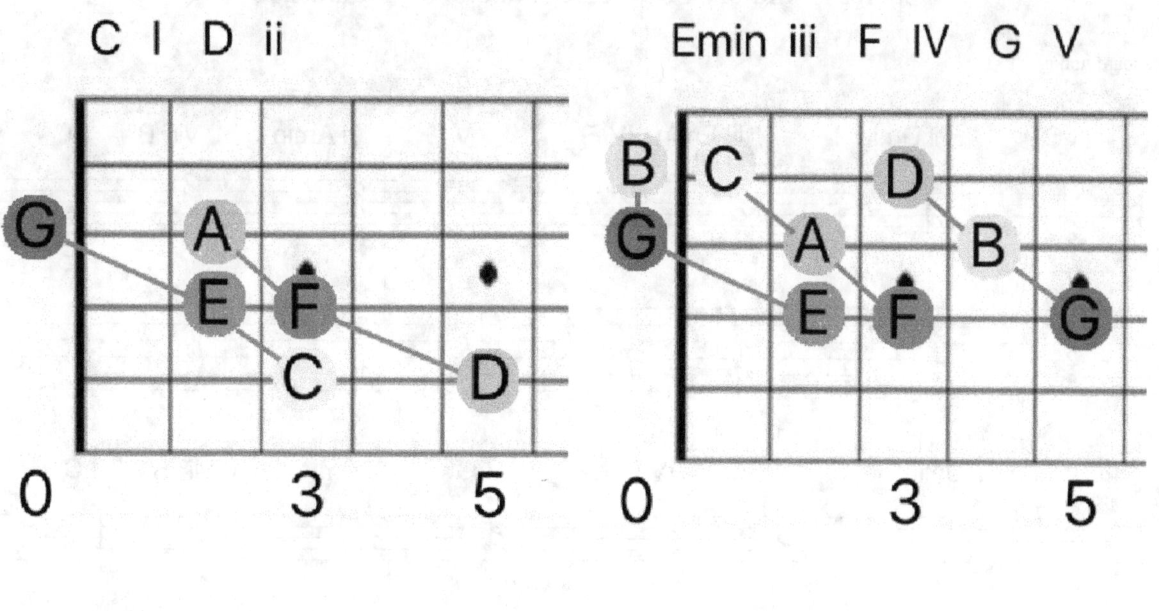

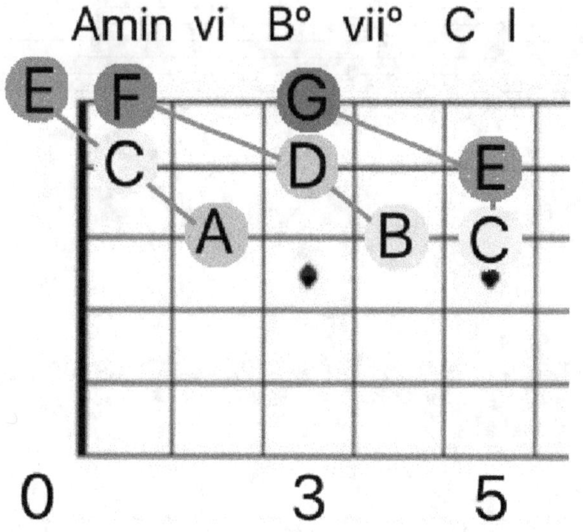

There is a way of spelling out these triads into formulas. Whenever we talk about a chord, we use diatonic intervals starting with the root as 1 and stack from there. So CEG = 1-3-5. Root + major third + perfect fifth.

Stacking from D, D = root, F = minor third, A = Perfect fifth. 1-*b*3-5. See how I added a *b* to *b*3? This is because we always use the major triad 135 as default. Anytime we have a deviation from 135 we have to label it so. Since F is 3 half-steps above D and not 4, we label it a *b*3, not a natural 3.

C Major Diatonic Triads

Roman numerals I=1 ii=2 iii=3 IV=4 V=5 vi=6 vii=7

Jared E. Davis

Uppercase=Major   Lowercase=Minor   ° = Diminished

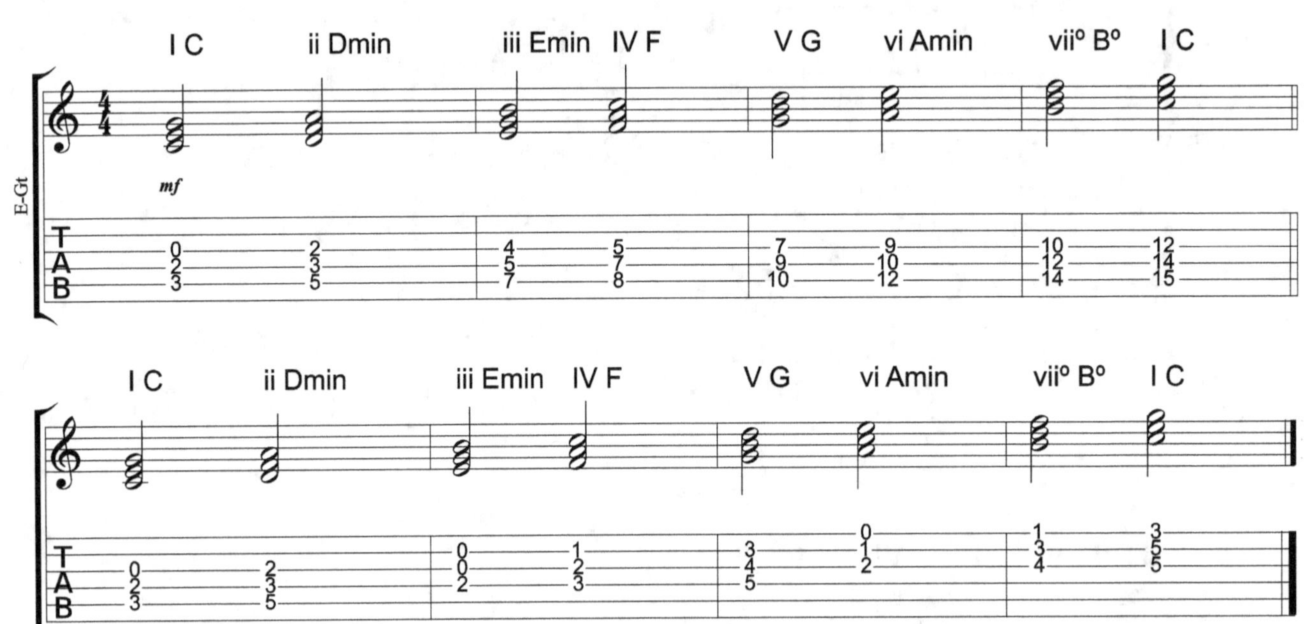

Major and minor chords both create a perfect fifth with the outside notes. The only difference between them is the middle note being a major or minor third.

vii° is a special chord. It's a weirdo you might say. It is the only chord that is not major or minor. It is built by stacking a minor third on top of a minor third. B-D is 3 half-steps and D-F is also 3 half-steps. That means the total number of half-steps is only 6, whereas all the other triads add up to 7.

The ° symbol stands for "diminished" we add this symbol to show that the third note (the 5th) is 1 half-step lower than normal to make a *b*5.

Diminished is a term that we only apply to certain intervals like fifths or sevenths. Usually, we have a perfect 5th with 7 half-steps. A diminished 5th would be 6 half-steps instead of 7. Same interval as a tritone.

Chromatic Triads

Although we can take triads from a scale, we can also just create triads from the chromatic scale. When we do this, there are only 4 types of them. Major, Minor, Diminished and Augmented. Let's go back to the single string theory.

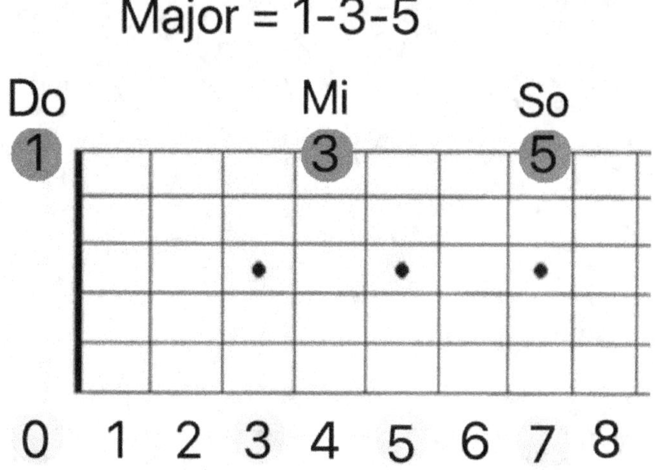

The major triad (135) is the parent of all triads. Just like the major scale is the parent scale of music. We label the intervals 135 because it comes from the scale degrees of the major scale.

Major Triads

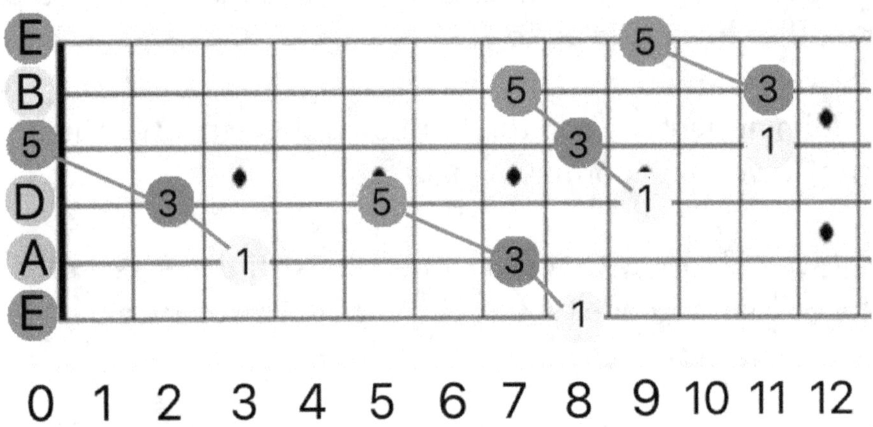

You can visualize the individual chromatic intervals as a minor third on top of a major third (4+3) or measure each note from the root, a major third and a perfect fifth. (3+7)

1 to 3 is 4-half steps (Maj 3)
3 to 5 is 3-half steps (Min 3)
1 to 5 is 7-half steps (P5)

Minor = 1-b3-5

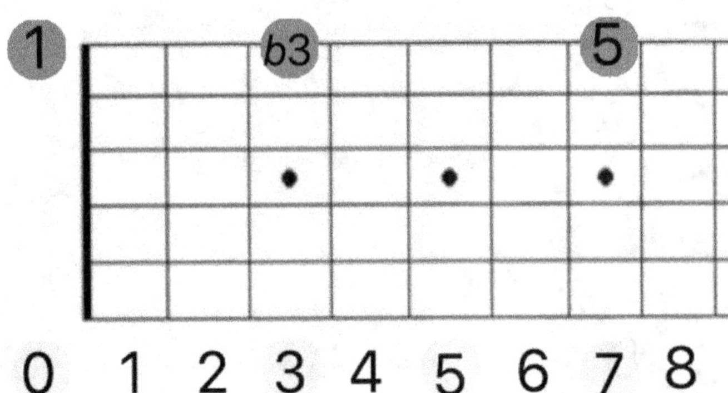

Minor triads (1-*b*3-5) have a flattened 3rd, but still keep the perfect fifth.

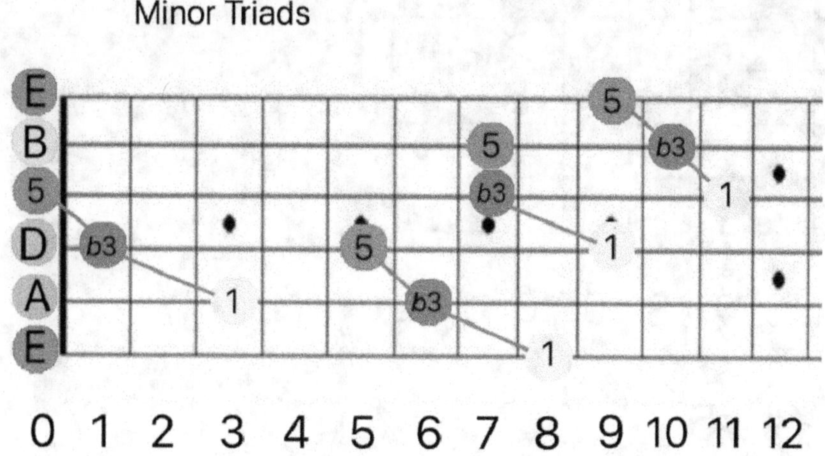

Visually it is the opposite of the major, major third on top of minor third. (3+4) but it still maintains the total distance of 7 half-steps from 1 to 5.

Diminished = 1-*b*3-*b*5

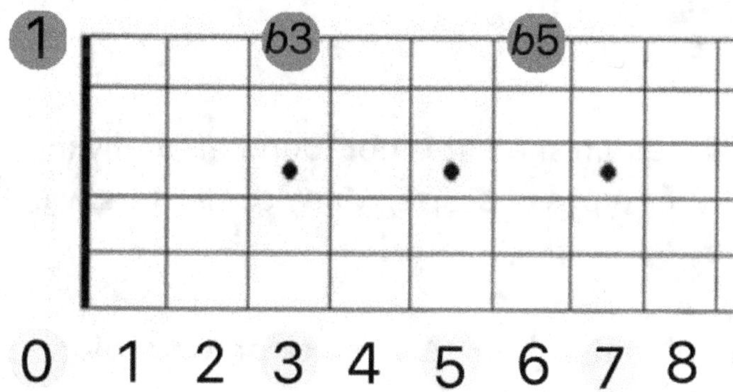

Diminished is a stack of two minor thirds with a total of 6-half steps from 1 to *b*5. (3+3).

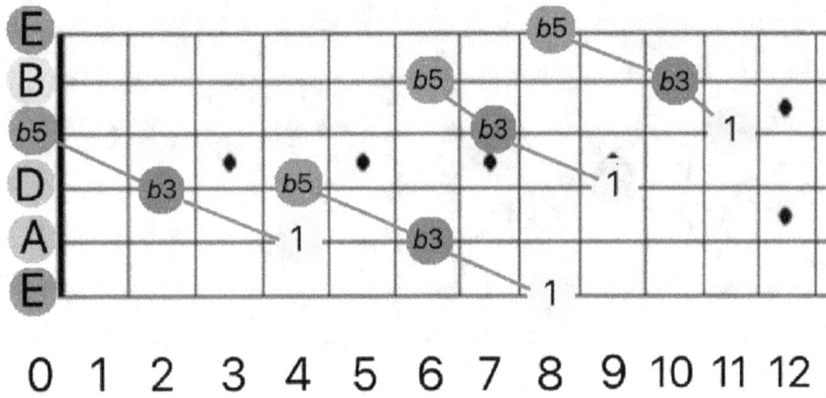

Augmented = 1-3-#5

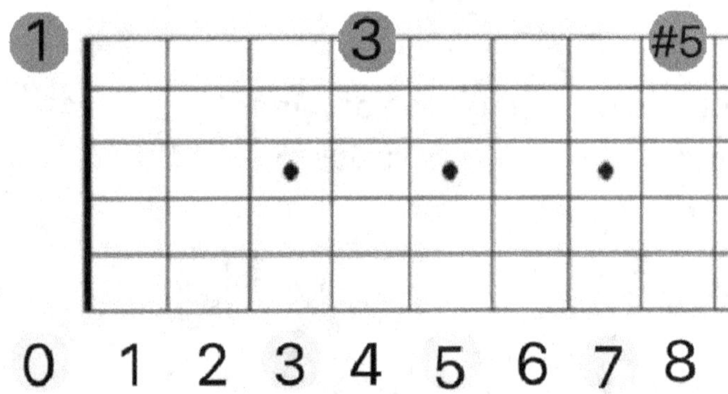

Augmented is another special chord like diminished. It is not found naturally in the major scale, but can be found in other types of scales. Many composers will use it in place of the V chord in a scale.

Augmented is somewhat the opposite of diminished. It is a stack of two major thirds with a total of 8-half steps from 1 to #5. (4+4)

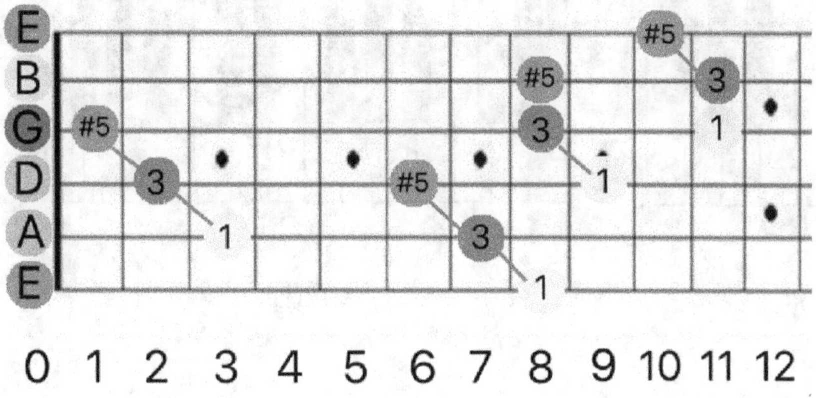

These formulas work the same way on paper and on the piano. Here we start on the note A, then we stack our third and fifth on top. A to C is a minor third (3 half-steps) and A to E is a perfect fifth (7 half-steps). Then all we have to do is adjust the 3 and 5 to make the other types of triads.

Notice on the A aug triad, we have an E#. This is one of the somewhat rare occasions in which, on paper, we can't use the note F because the letter F would be a fourth away from C#. We want to make sure our stack is only in thirds. Of course, on your instrument, E# is the same note as F.

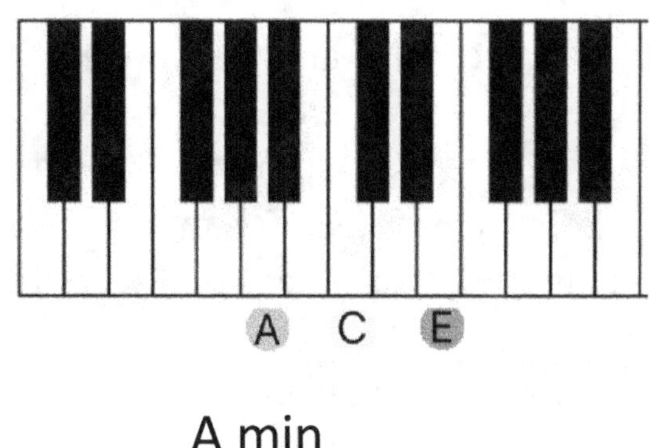

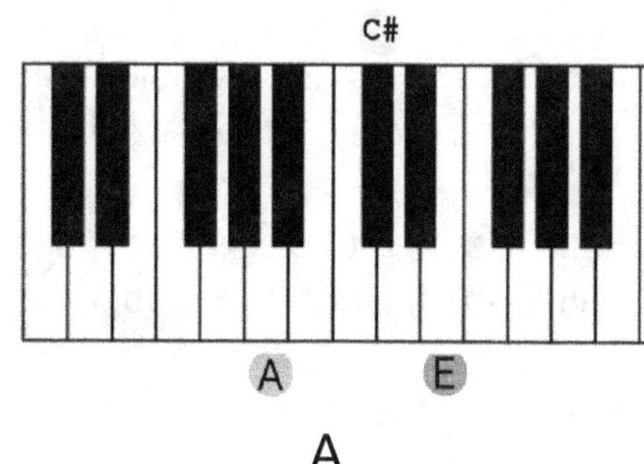

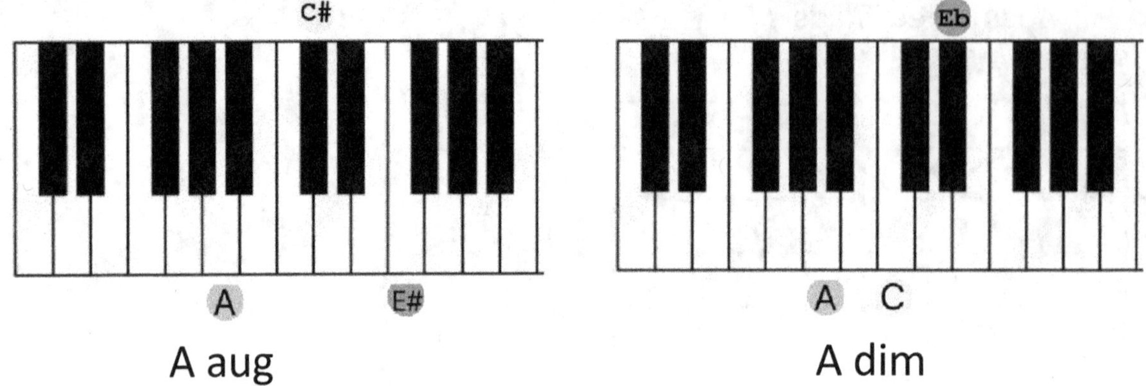

Lesson 3: Review

Each string is tuned a Perfect fourth or 5 half-steps away from each other, except for the G-B strings which are tuned a major third or 4 half-steps away.

All intervals, chords and scale shapes will be altered by 1 fret if the B string is included.

You can create interval shapes on two adjacent strings, or by skipping over a string for larger intervals. Just be sure to count the half-steps in each shape.

There are many different ways to play a major scale. You must not only memorize the notes of C major, but also memorize the different shapes to play the scale.

Using the notes of C major, we can make 3 note chords from each scale degree by stacking in thirds. These are the diatonic triads. Seven notes in a scale means there are seven triads. Remember I IV V are major, ii iii vi are minor and vii is diminished.

Learn to play the triads of C major horizontally and vertically, and memorize which notes are in each triad. Ex: ii = D F A

Learn the formulas to create each triad type. 1 3 5 is major, 1 b3 5 is minor, 1 b3 b5 is diminished, and 1 3 #5 is augmented. Then learn those shapes on the guitar.

Whatever note the 1 is on, that note will be the letter name of your chord.

Lesson 4: Chords-Keys-Movable Units

This whole concept of deriving diatonic chords from a major scale is what the term "Key" means. Whichever note you start your scale with is the name of the key you are in. That's why C major scale starts with the note C.

We have only been talking about the key of C so far, however we can start the major scale with any of the 12 notes. Which means there are 12 different major keys. Each key will have the same order of diatonic chords and still use the WWHWWWH scale pattern.

When you start the major scale pattern on a different note than C, you will end up having sharps or flats in your scale. Let's do our major scale pattern from F and G to see what happens.

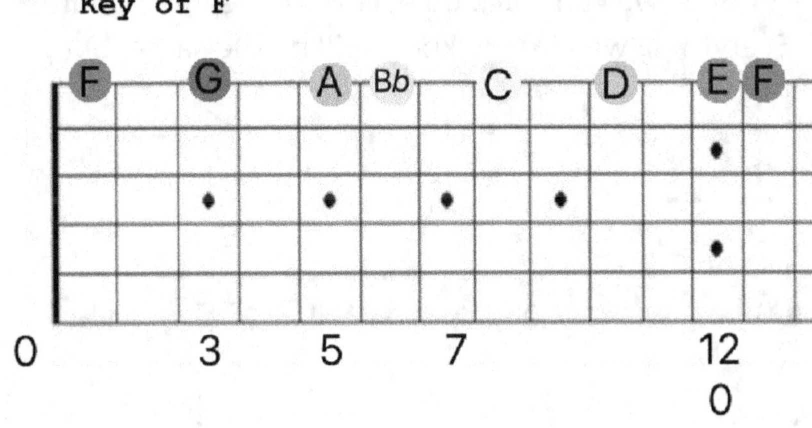

As you can see, we only had to change one note. B became B*b*. That means the key of F has only one flat (B*b*) and all other notes are the same as C major. So, all you have to do is play B*b* instead of B in your C major scale and you will be in F.

Key of G

Now starting our pattern from G, we get B natural back, but add F# instead of F. Which means the key of G only has one sharp (F#). You can do exactly as we did before, play the C major scale and change F to F#. This is all you have to do to be in the key of G. Whatever note you start on is the new Do/1 of the 7-note scale. So, key of G: G=Do/1 A=Re/2 B=Mi/3 etc. - Key of F: F=Do/1 G=Re/2 A=Mi/3 etc.

Then once we find the correct notes, we can stack up each scale degree in thirds and find our diatonic triads. Everything we already know will be the same, but shifted to the new starting note F or G.

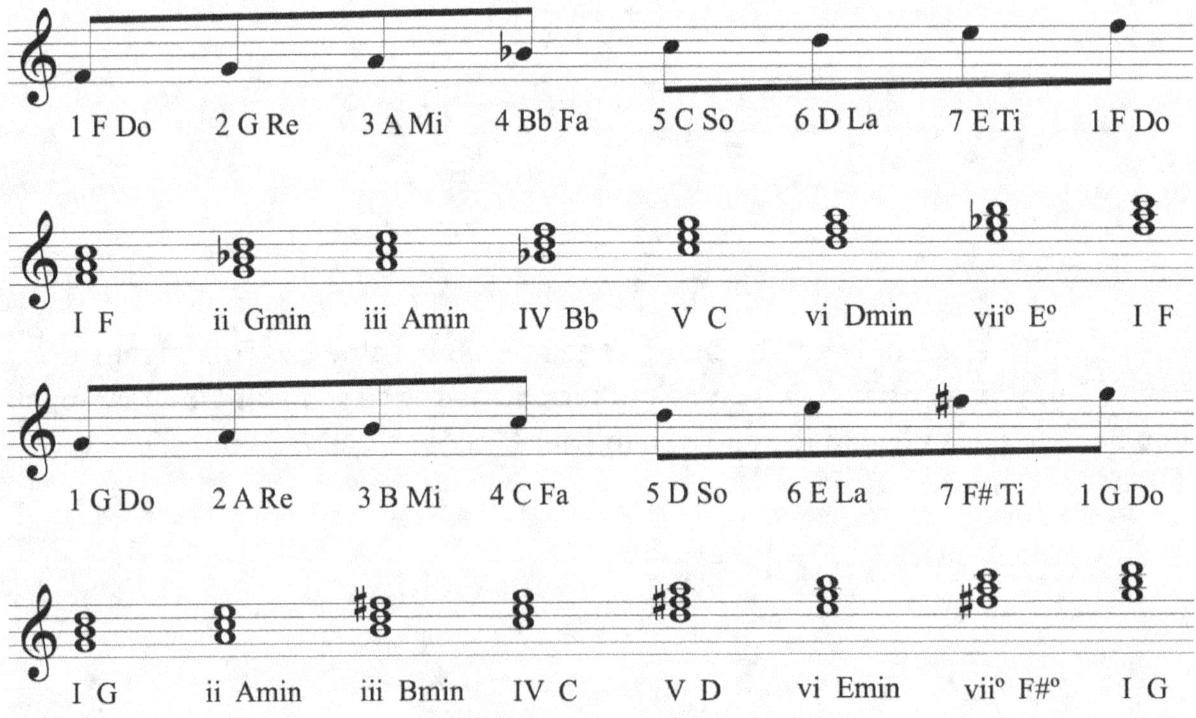

Circle of 5ths

It can be a lot to remember which keys have sharps or flats, and how many sharps or flats. This is where the circle of fifths can come in handy as a visual tool.

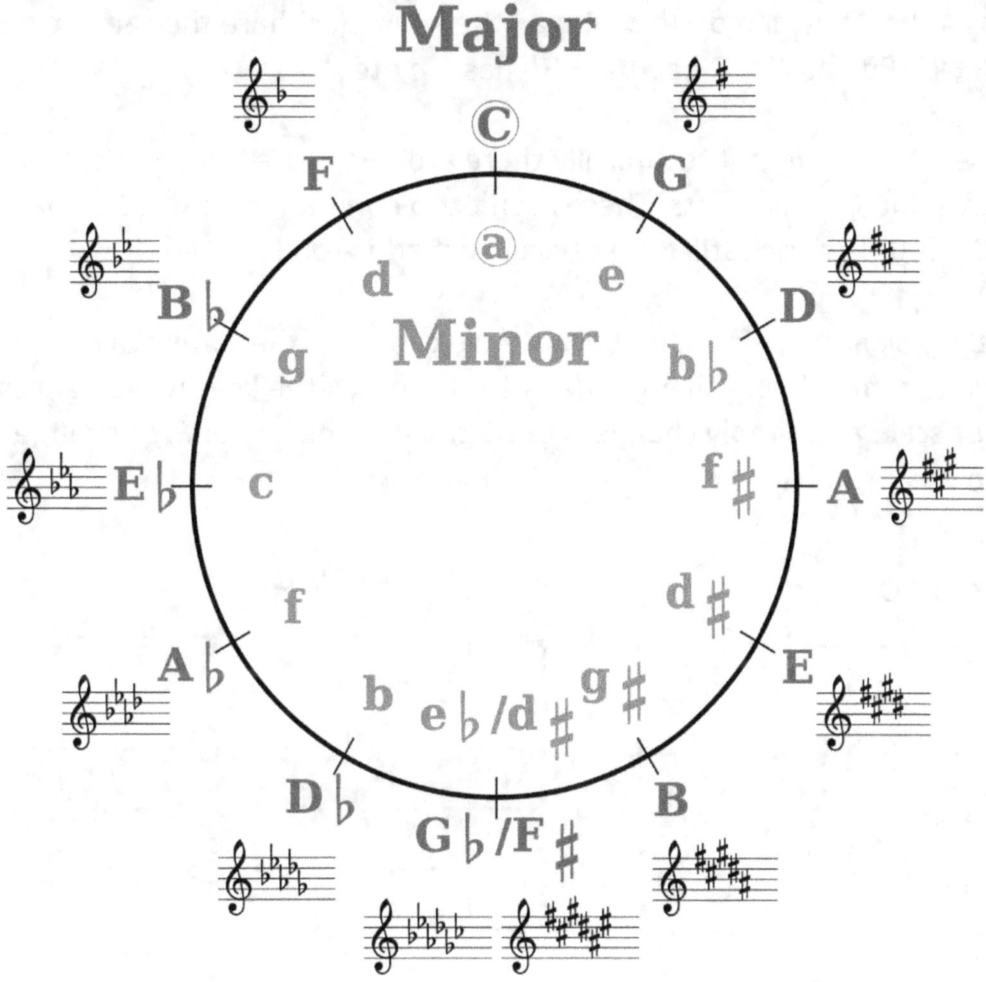

I know it looks crazy, but it's easier to understand than it looks.
Going clockwise (right) the notes move by perfect 5ths, and going counter clockwise (left) the notes move by perfect 4ths.

That's where the name circle of 5ths comes from. This is a tool to help you find how many sharps or flats are in any key. Clockwise adds sharps and counter clockwise adds flats. They meet on the opposite side at G*b*/F# where we get 6 of either sharps or flats (depending on which key you call it, G*b* or F#).

The order of sharps is FCGDAEB and the order of flats is BEADGCF.
Meaning the first sharp is F# in the key of G and first flat is B*b* in the key of F. There is also a cool trick that can help you remember how many sharps or flats a key has. The number 7 is the trick. The key of A has 3 sharps – which means the key of A*b* has 4 flats. You can do this with all the keys that share the same letter name. E has 3 # – E*b* has 4 *b*, G has 1 # – G*b* has 6 *b* etc...

This chart doesn't show it, but technically there are two more, C# and C*b*.
C# has 7 sharps and C*b* has 7 flats. These aren't too common, but since C# has 7 sharps and C has 0. The trick still works because it adds to 7!

Knowing the key signatures is useful because we can keep the same scale fingering or shape and simply change the notes to match the key signature. I can play a C major scale and simply change B to B*b* to be in the key of F, or change F to F# to be in the key of G.

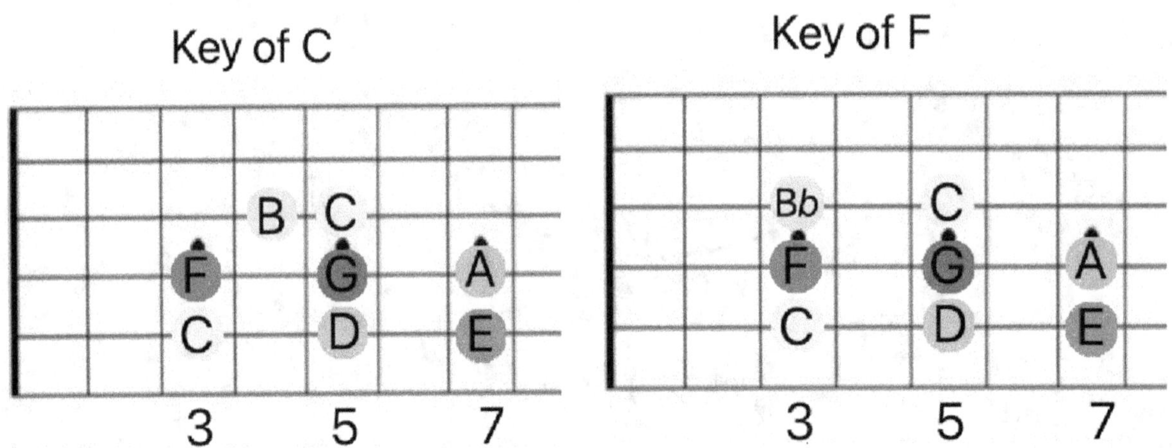

Minor Keys of Circle

The inner circle refers to the minor keys that share the same amount of accidentals as the major keys on the outside of the circle.

We call them "Relative Minors". For example, the Key of A minor has no accidentals just like the key of C major. You can easily find the relative minor key to a major key because it is based on the vi chord. A minor is the vi chord in C. More on this later.

For now, let's get back to some notes. There are only two more things to memorize in order to have the whole neck finished.

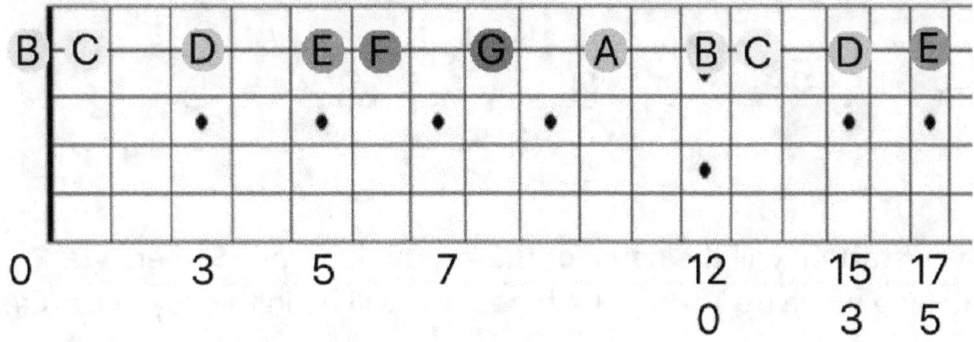

Memorize the B string, the last of the 6 strings. Also, you can memorize this position from 5th fret to 10th fret.

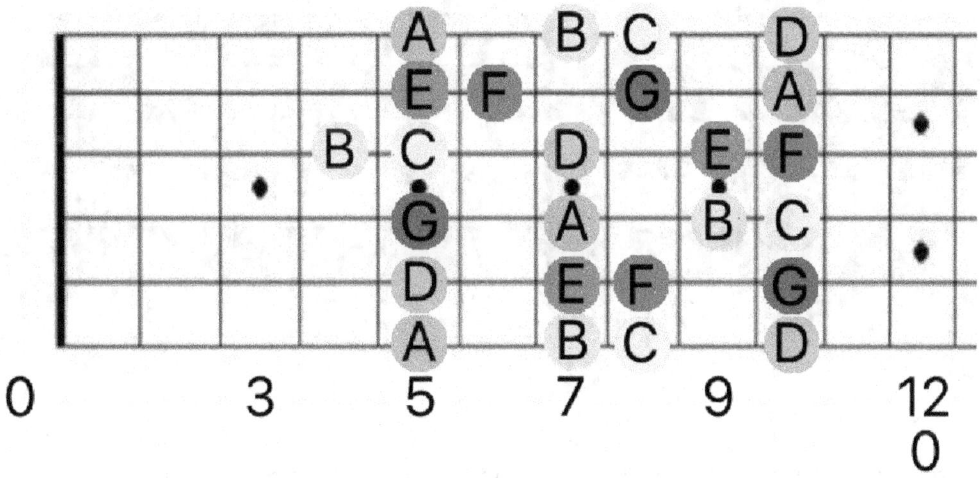

Movable Chords and Scales

Take a look at this major scale pattern from earlier. Now forget the note names and just think of it as 1-7 scale degrees and what the shape/pattern is.

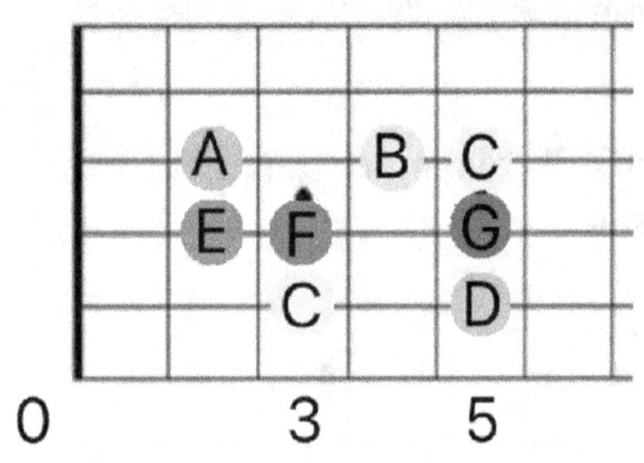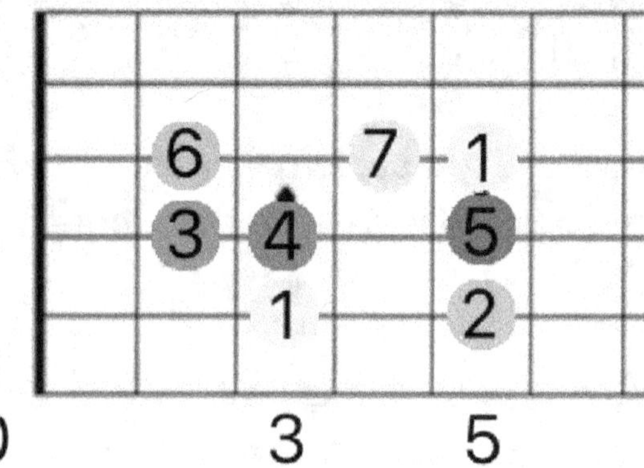

Whatever note you start on will the name of the key/major scale. So here we started on C, but if we move up 1 fret (1 half-step) we will be in the key of D*b*/C#.

If we move up another half-step, or whole-step from C, we start on the note D at the 5th fret. Which means we will be in the key of D or have a D major scale.

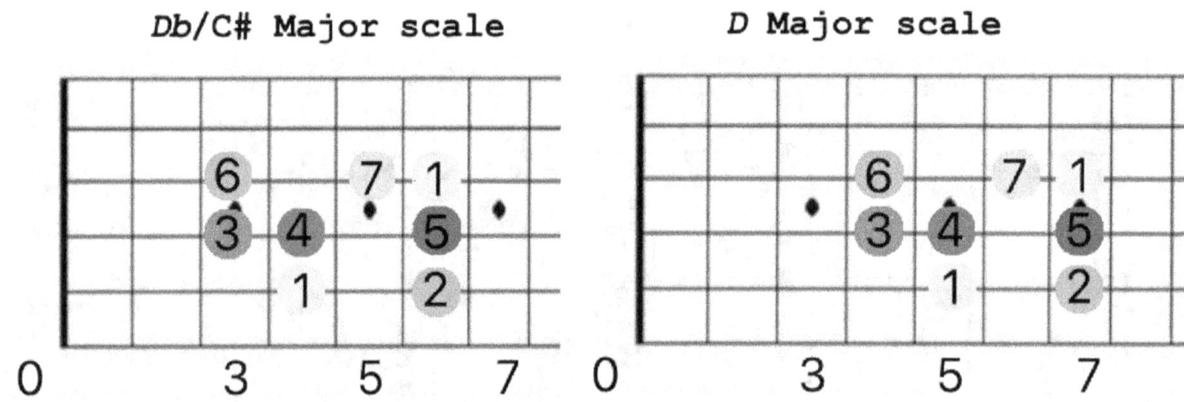

All we do is relate the scale pattern/shape to a starting note on the A string. You can do this with any shape/pattern/scale.
You may have heard of "bar chords", which refers to chord shapes that require you to bar the strings with your index finger. Personally, I prefer to call them movable chords because not all of them require an actual bar.

6 Major Scale Position Fingerings

C major scale

Jared E. Davis

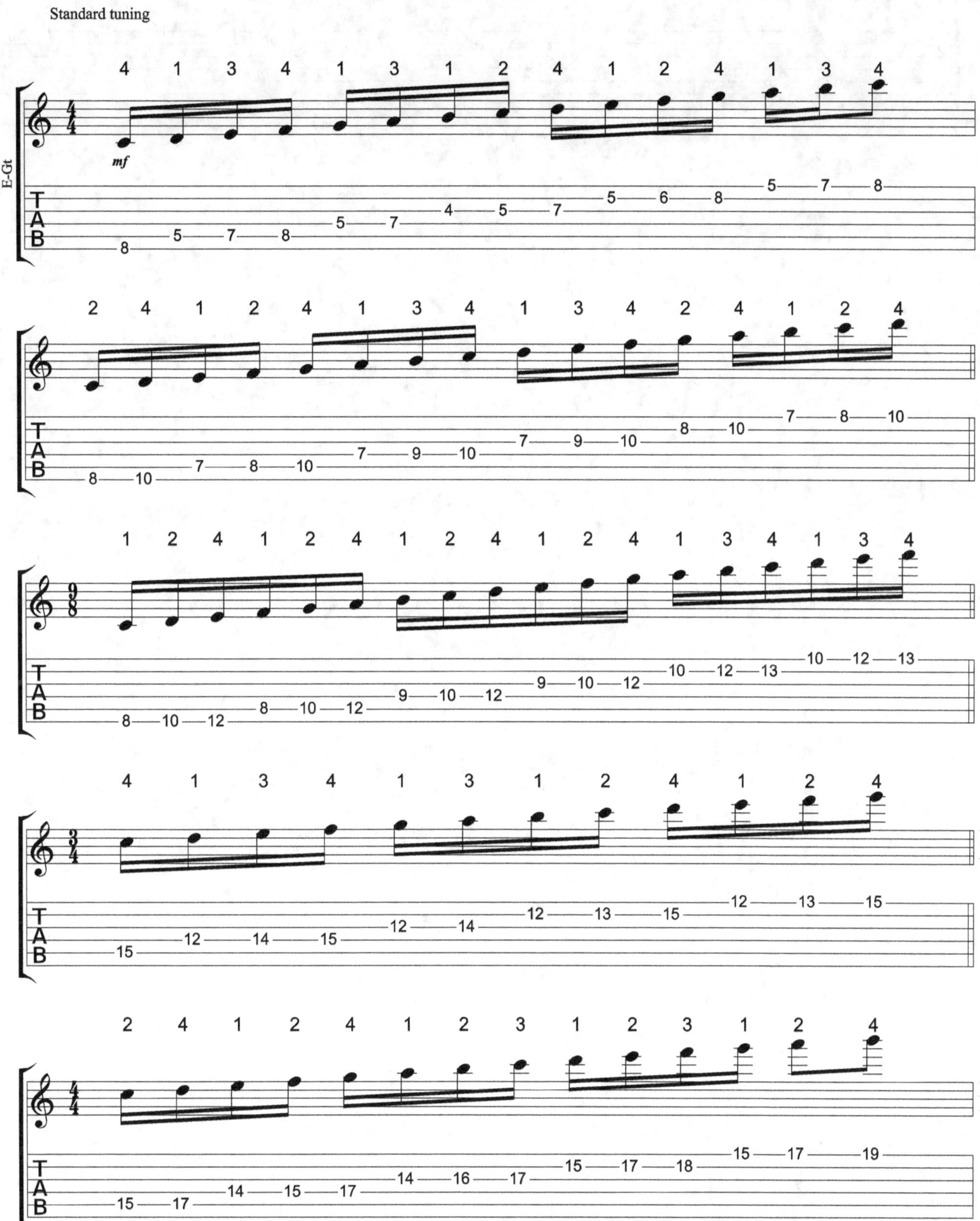

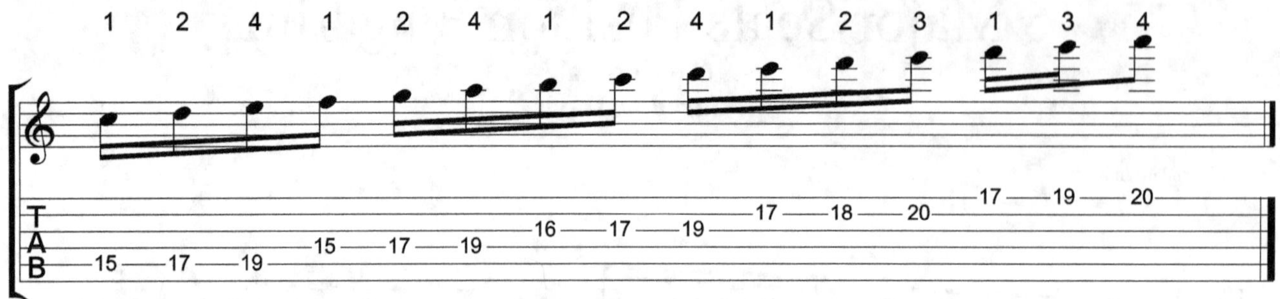

1   2   4   1   2   4   1   2   4   1   2   3   1   3   4
15   17   19   15   17   19   16   17   19   17   18   20   17   19   20

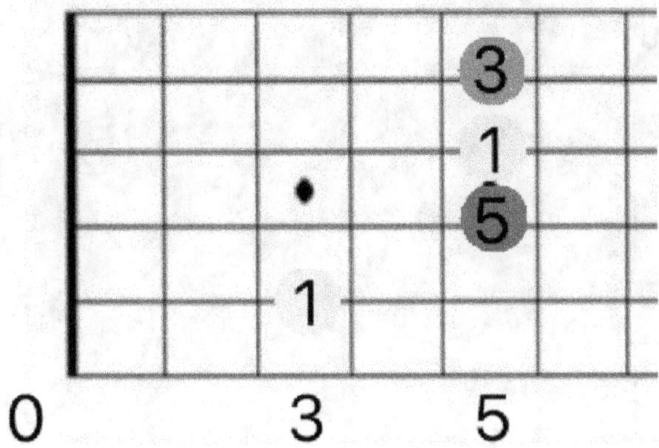

Here is a basic major triad (1-3-5) movable chord shape. Since the note on the A string is C, it is a C major chord. 1-3-5 does not have to be in order to make the triad and you can repeat notes like we did with the 1.

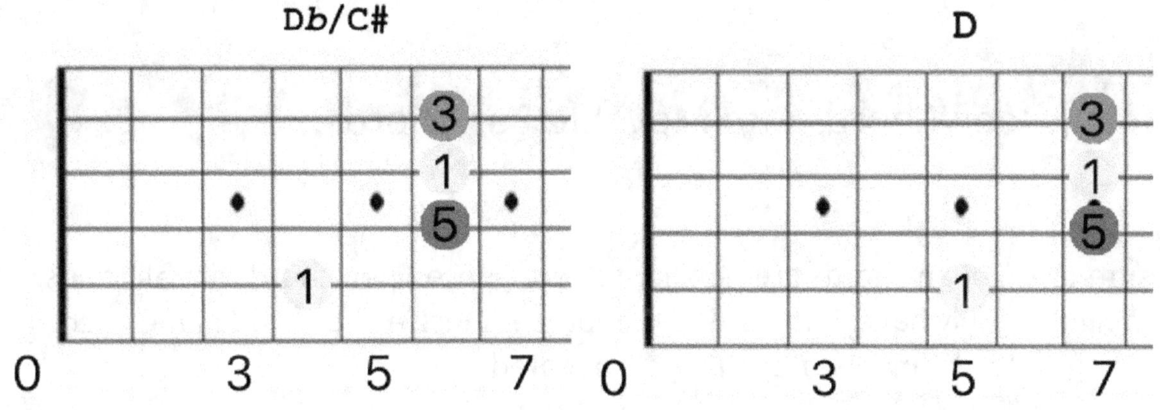

If we move this major chord up by 1 fret (1 half-step) it becomes a D♭/C# major chord. If we move it up another fret or whole-step from C, it becomes a D major chord. You can do this with any chord shape and move 1 to any note on a string.

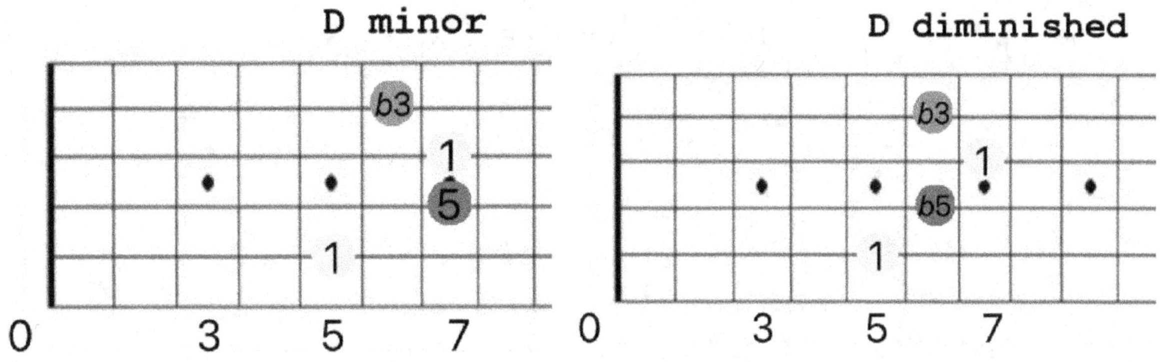

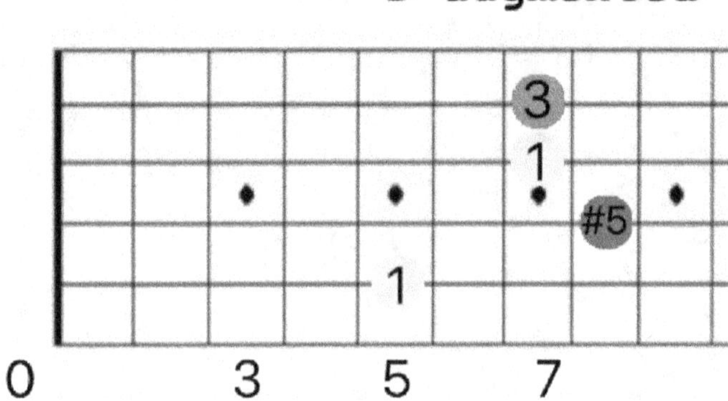

The same interval construction works for these shapes of triads. You can raise or lower each chord tone to make other types of chords, and they will all still be movable. Whatever note the 1 is on will be the letter name of the chord.

Turning Open Chords into Movable Bar Chords

I'm sure these open chords are familiar to you. These open chords are all triads, meaning they only have 3 notes. See for yourself! Pick a chord and name each note, you will only find 3 notes that get repeated.

These shapes are all actually movable. All you have to do is keep the same shape and imagine your index finger is the nut where the open string notes are.

Take a look at what happens when we move each of these shapes up one fret and bar the 1st fret with our index finger. Each shape remains the same, but the note name goes up by one half-step. This is how a Capo works as well.

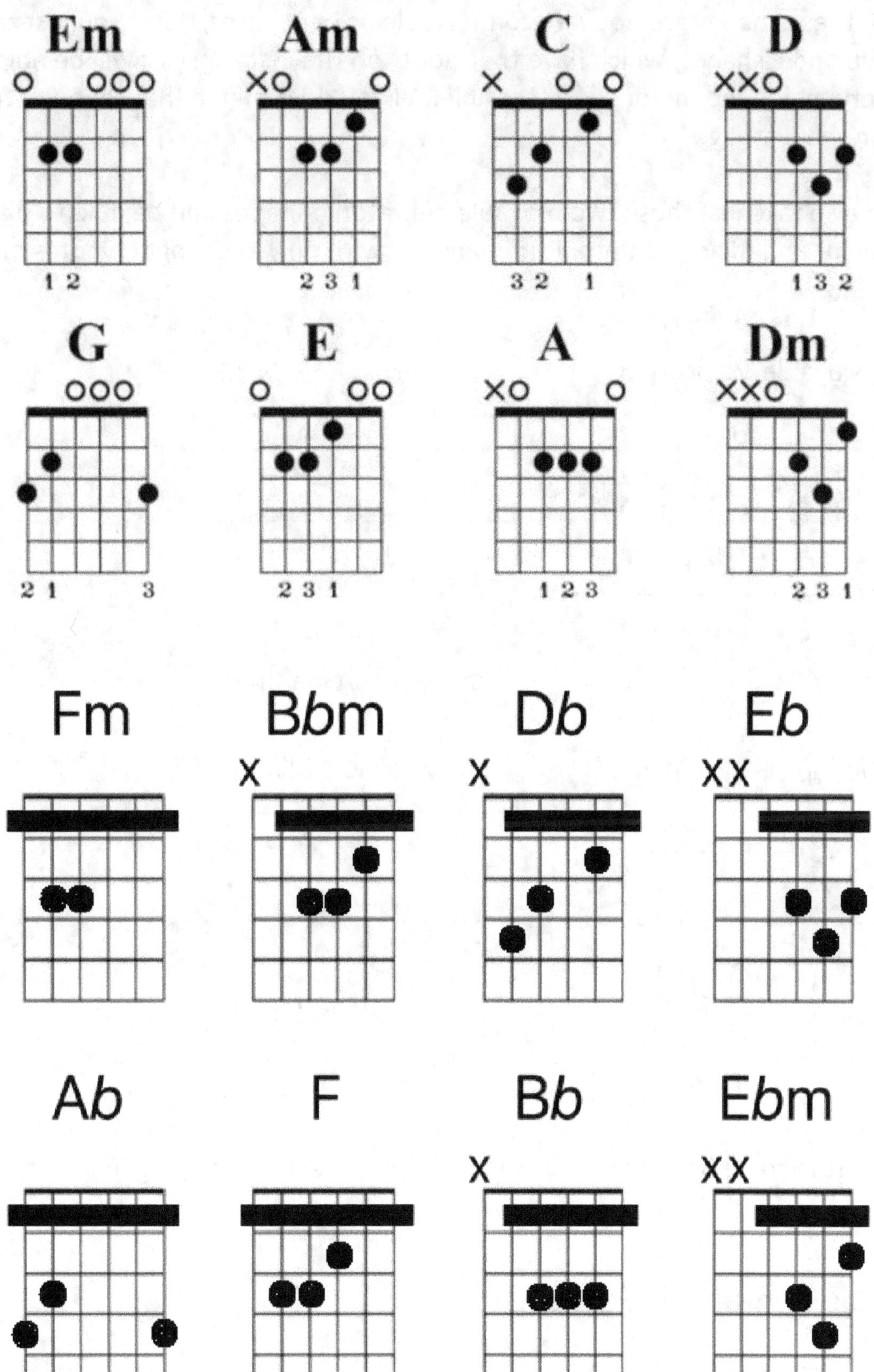

Em
Am
C
D
G
E
A
Dm
Fm
Bbm
Db
Eb
Ab
F
Bb
Ebm

Some of these shapes are not very comfortable as bar chords, but if you just take the E min and E shapes, which have their roots on the E-string, you will be able to play every major and minor chord possible. All you do is match that shape to the notes on the E-string.

You can also take just these two movable pentatonic shapes and be able to play every major and minor pentatonic possible. All with only knowing the notes on the E-string.

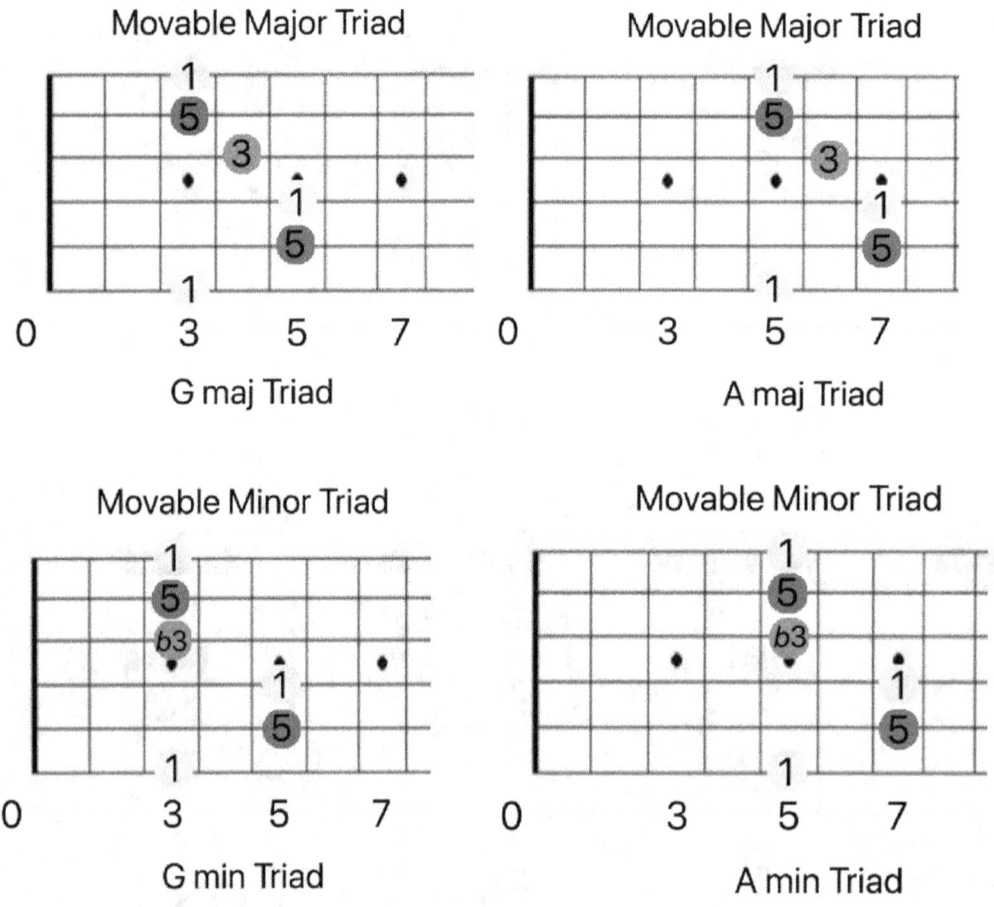

Each of these come from the E and E min open shape. Each require an index bar.

Movable Pentatonic Patterns

Then, if you pair the major and minor chord shapes to the pentatonic shapes, you can pretty much play over every song in existence.

Minor Pentatonic

Major Pentatonic

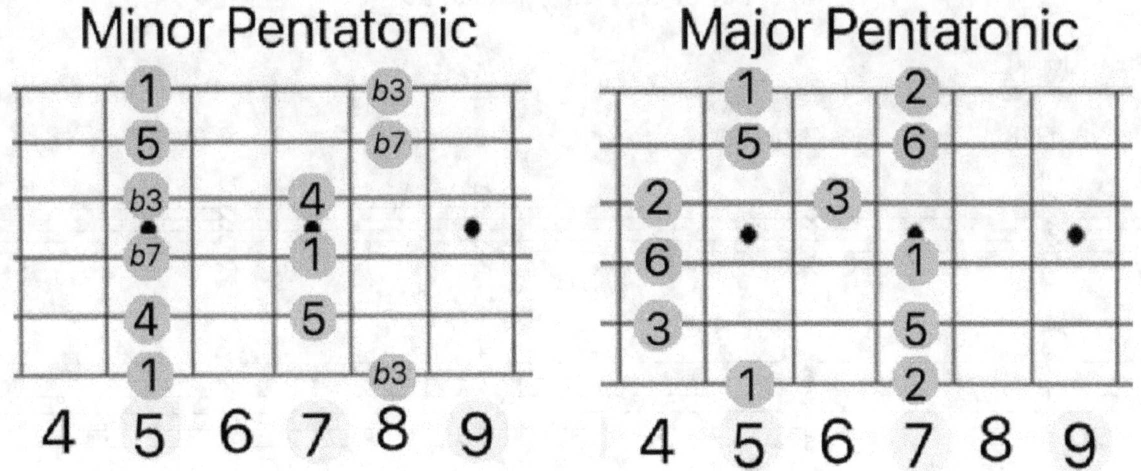

Since these shapes start on the 5th fret of the E-string, they will be A minor and A major pentatonic patterns. Move your E and E min shapes to the 5th fret to match the chords to the pentatonic scale. Those E shapes will then have the 5th fret note as their root, which is the note A, so they will become A and A min chords.

Diminished Pentatonic

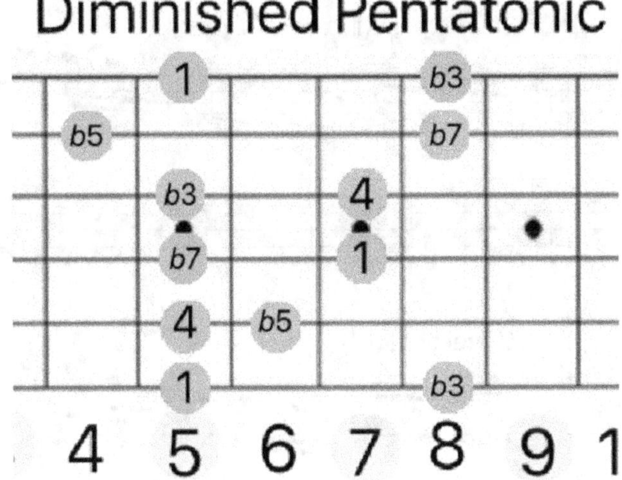

There is also a diminished or minor *b5* pentatonic shape. You can pair this with that pesky vii chord in a major key or any diminished/half-dim/min-7*b5* chord.

Take a look at how we can use these shapes to play in a key.

Matching Triads to Pentatonics in a Key (E string root)

key of G triads + pentatonics

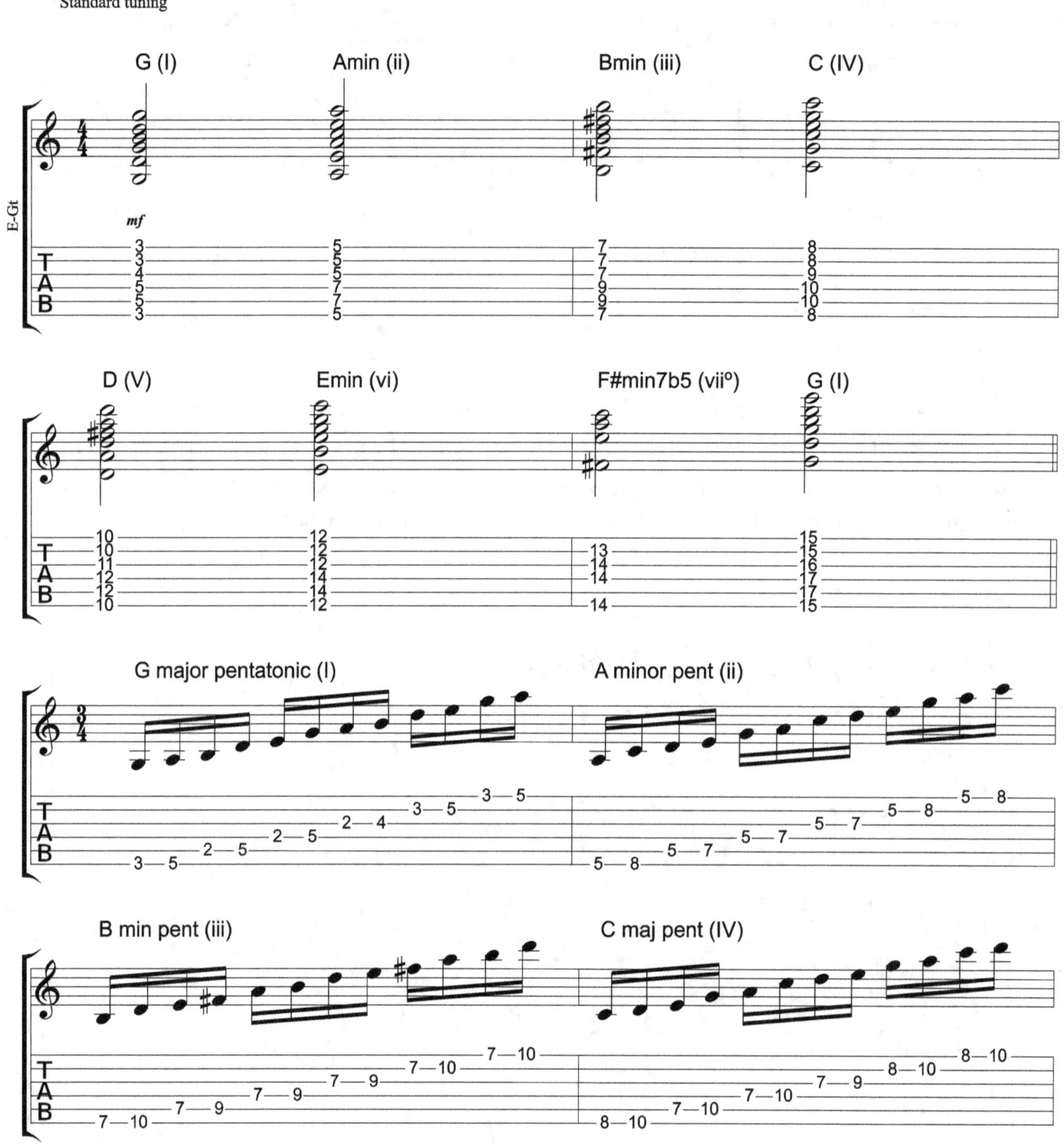

D maj pent (V)
E min pent (vi)

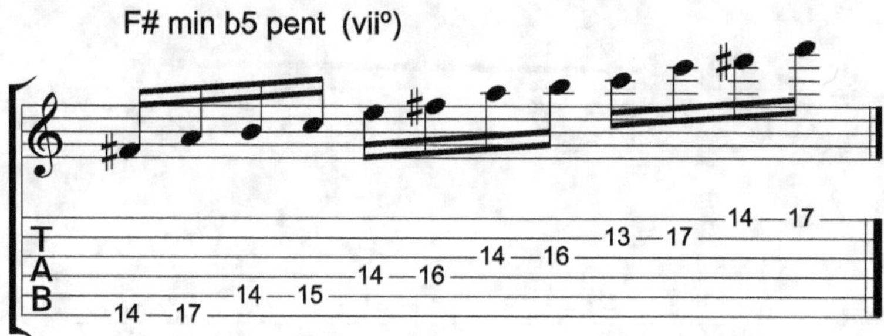

F# min b5 pent (vii°)

Modes of Major Scale

Another thing we derive from the major scale is modes. Modes are basically the other 7 note scales we get from starting at each scale degree of the major scale. Since there are 7 scale degrees, we get 7 different modes.

Each of the modes have a unique pattern of whole and half-steps like the major scale does. The best way to learn the construction of each mode is to compare the scale degrees to the major mode. Just like we did with chords.

If we take the pattern from each mode and move them to all start on the note C, we can add sharps or flats to the scale degrees that get altered. Again, we use the major scale 1 2 3 4 5 6 7 as the default and add sharps or flats to make changes.

C Ionian 1 2 3 4 5 6 7

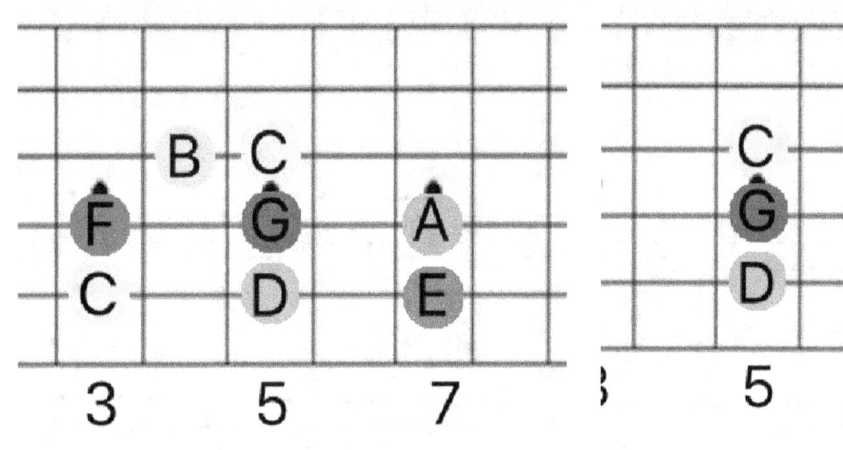

D Dorian 1 2 b3 4 5 6 b7

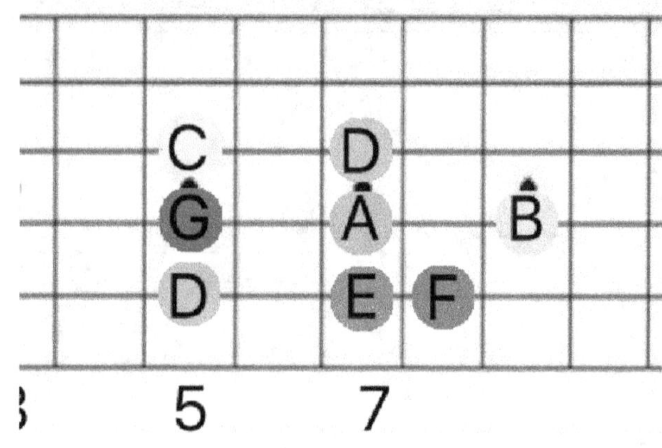

E Phrygian 1 b2 b3 4 5 b6 b7

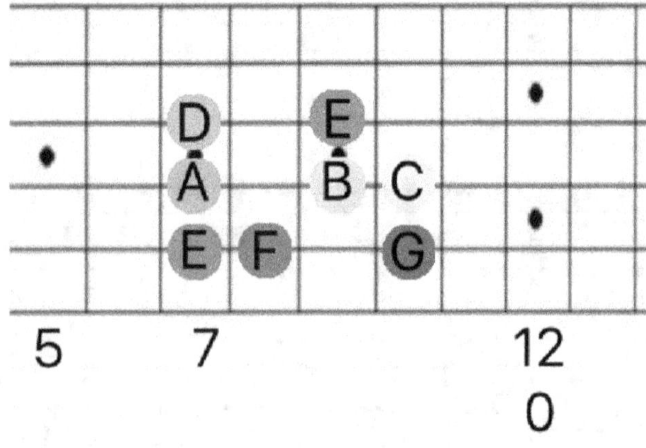

F Lydian 1 2 3 #4 5 6 7

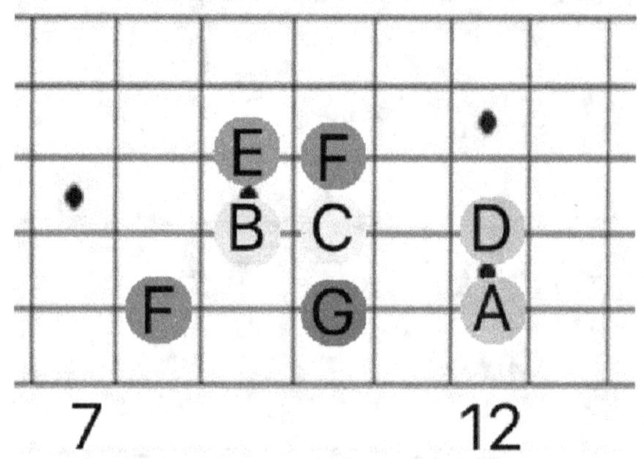

G Mixolydian 1 2 3 4 5 6 b7

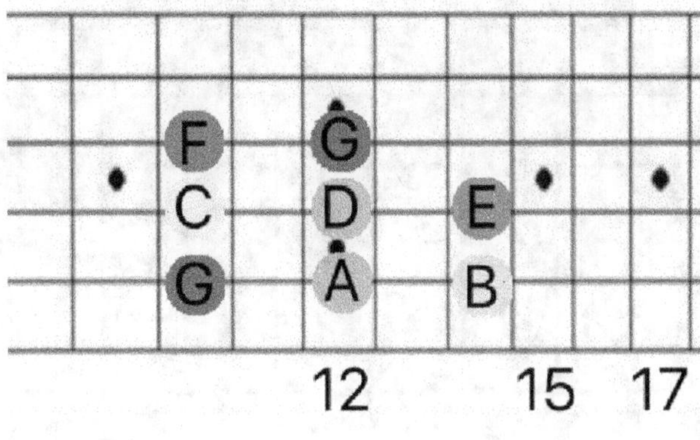

A Aeolian 1 2 b3 4 5 b6 b7

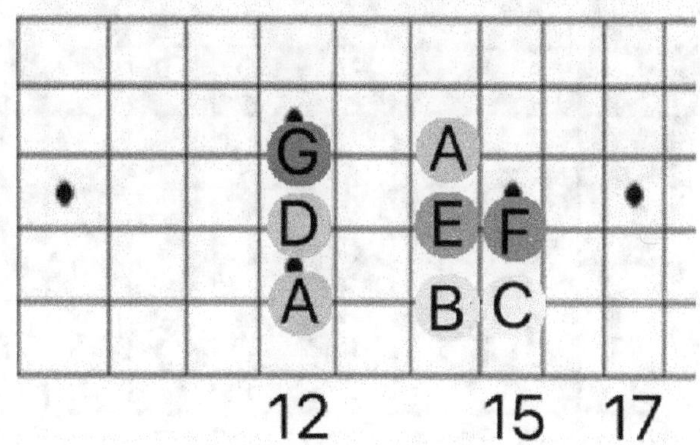

B Locrian 1 b2 b3 4 b5 b6 b7

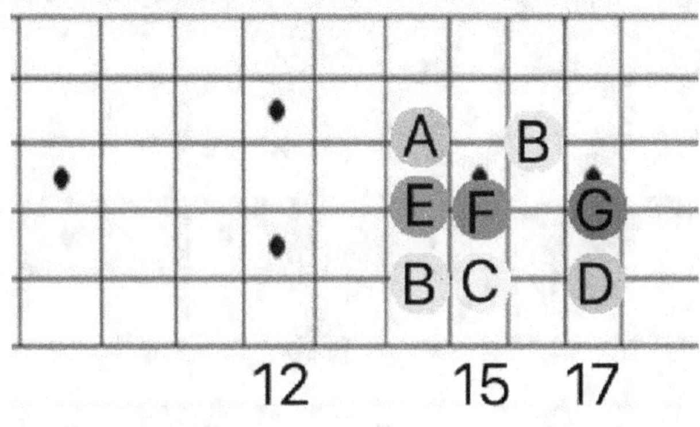

By following the notes of C major from each scale degree, we can learn the shapes and altered scale degrees for each mode. Then we can move those shapes to start on the note C to visualize the altered scale degrees.

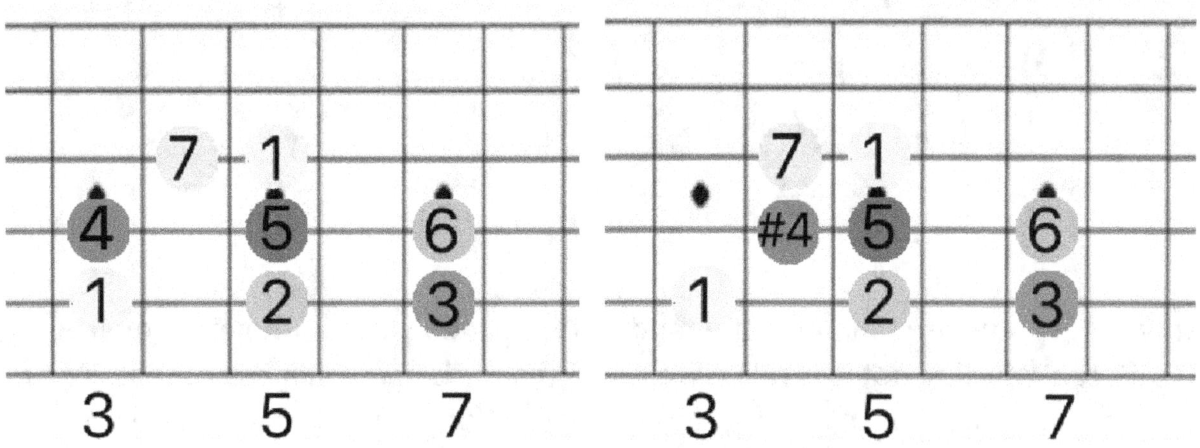

C Mixolydian 1 2 3 4 5 6 b7   C Dorian 1 2 b3 4 5 6 b7

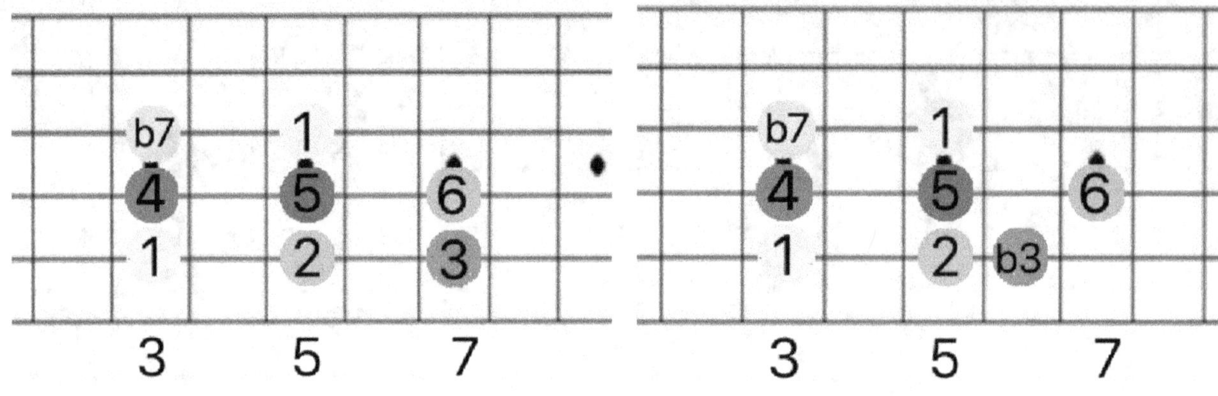

C Aeolian 1 2 b3 4 5 b6 b7   C Phrydian 1 b2 b3 4 5 b6 b7

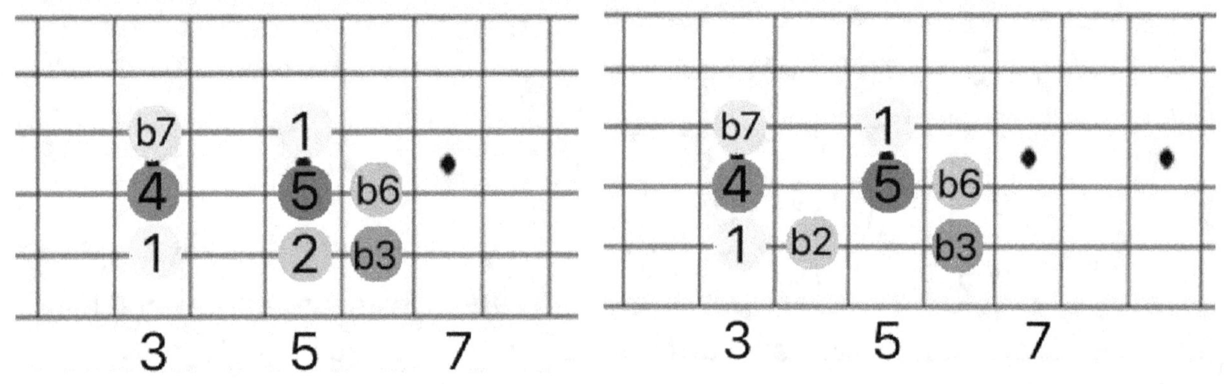

C Locrian 1 b2 b3 4 b5 b6 b7

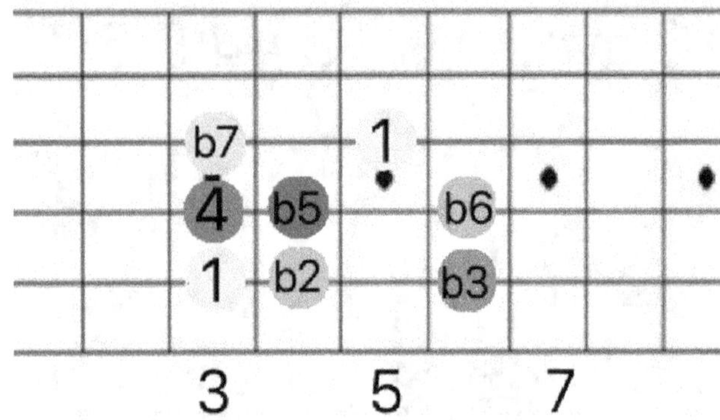

Now that you understand how the modes are formed you can move them around
to different starting notes just like we do with chords and other scales. You just
have to remember which mode goes with each chord. 7 modes = 7 chords

7th Chords – Sus Chords – Tensions

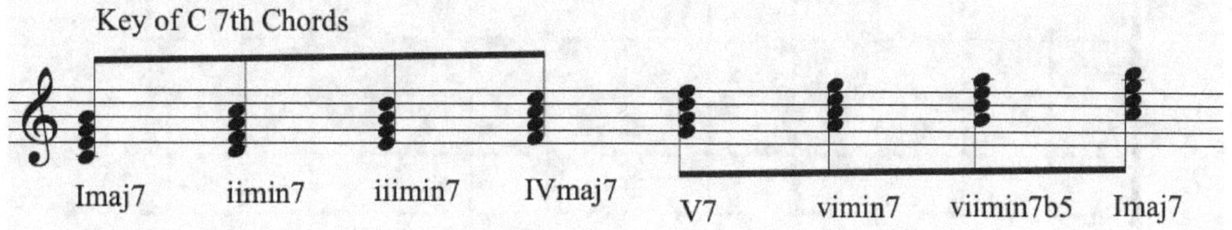

7th chords are what we get when we stack another third on top of the triads. So, instead of just 3 notes of 1 3 5, we get 4 notes 1 3 5 7.

You can see how the roman numeral chord labels get changed to add the 7th. There are only 4 different types of 7th chords we get from the major scale.

Maj7 1 3 5 7   Min7 1 b3 5 b7

Dom7 1 3 5 b7   Half-Diminished or Min7b5. 1 b3 b5 b7

Let's look at them on a single string to visualize their differences within the 12-note chromatic scale. Remember a major 3rd is 4 half steps, P5 is 7 and major 7th is 11. You can see that clearly matches up with the fret numbers like we did before.

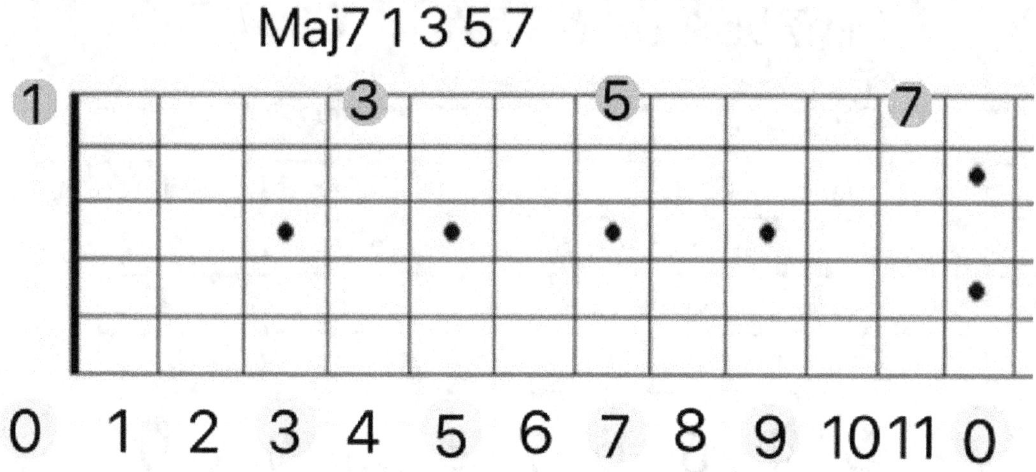

Dom7 1 3 5 *b7*

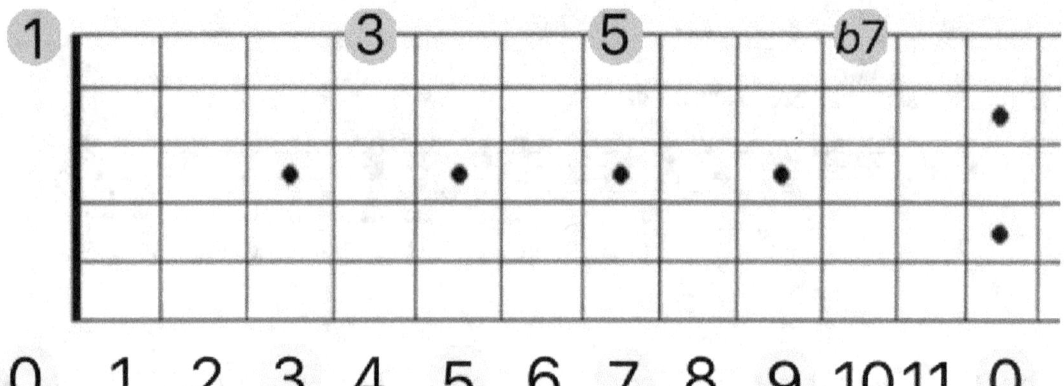

Min7 1 *b3* 5 *b7*

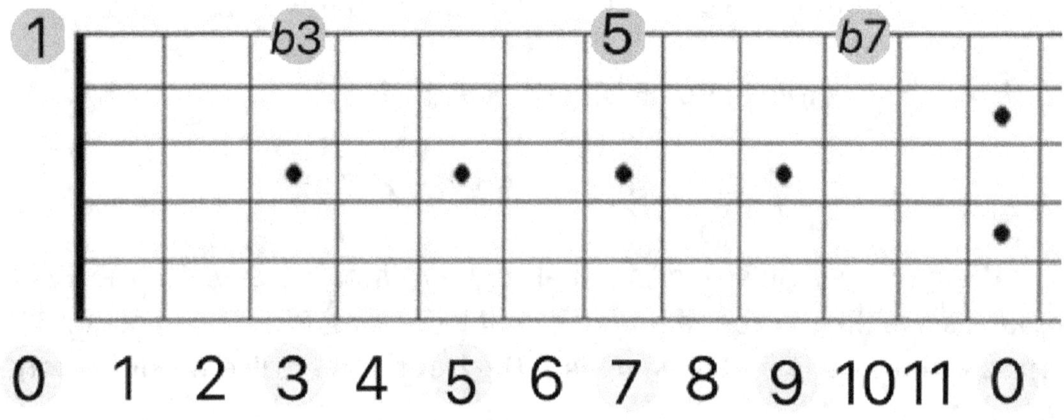

Min7*b5* 1 *b3* *b5* *b7*

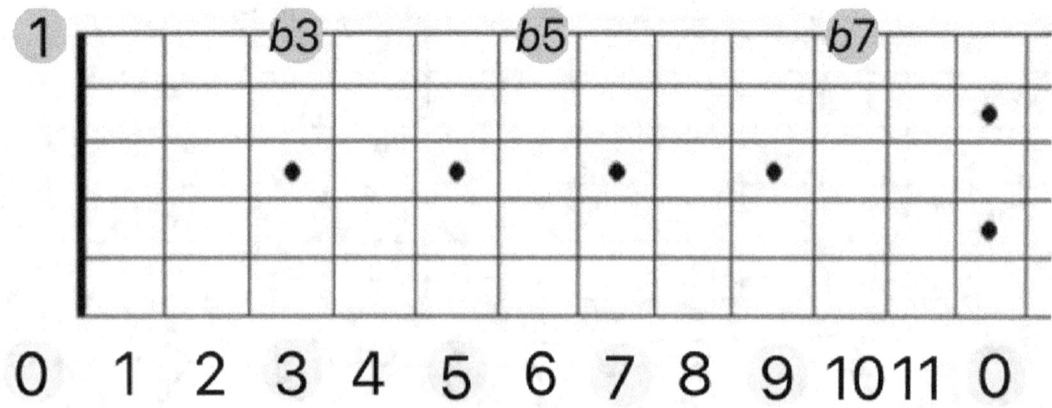

Key of C Diatonic 7th Chords
A string root

Standard tuning

E-Gt

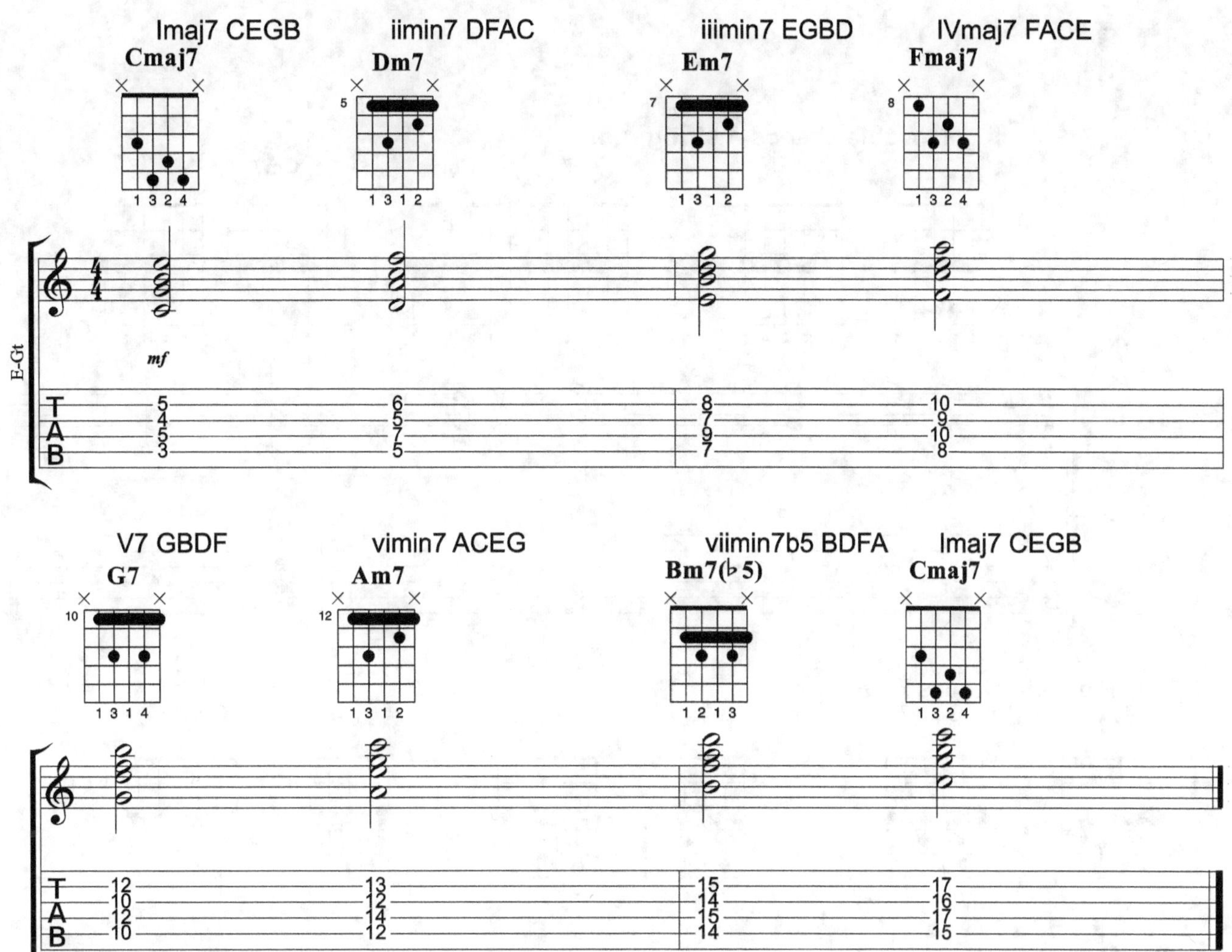

Movable Chords for E and A string roots

Maj Maj7 Dom7 - Min Min7 Min7b5 (halfdim)

Jared E. Davis

Connect the shapes to the note on string

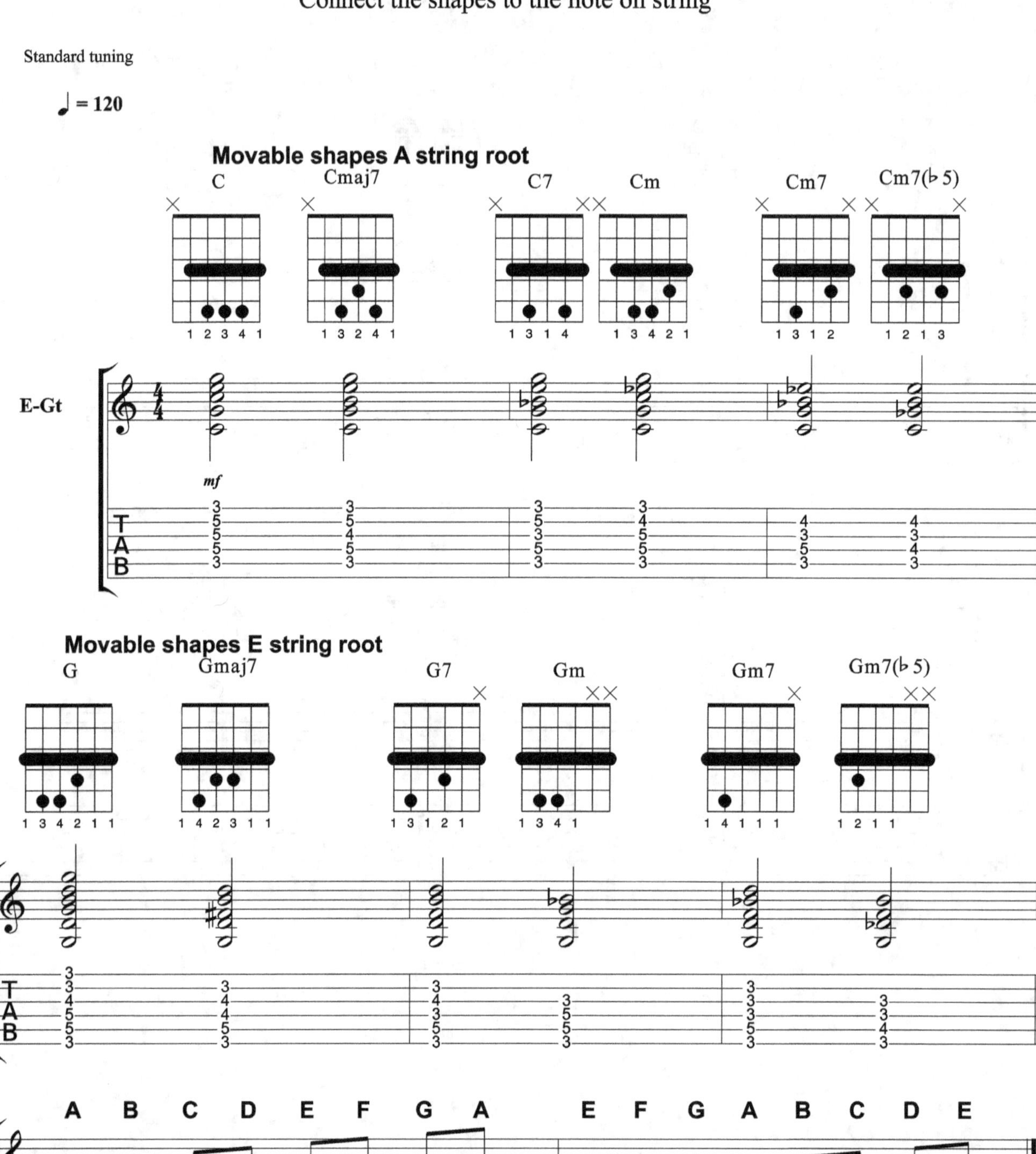

It is necessary to learn each of these shapes from A string roots and E string roots.
Memorize these shapes and practice moving them to different root notes.

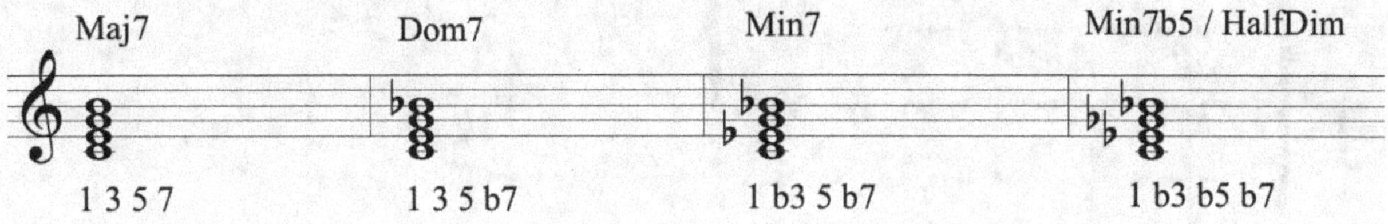

Sus 2 – Sus 4

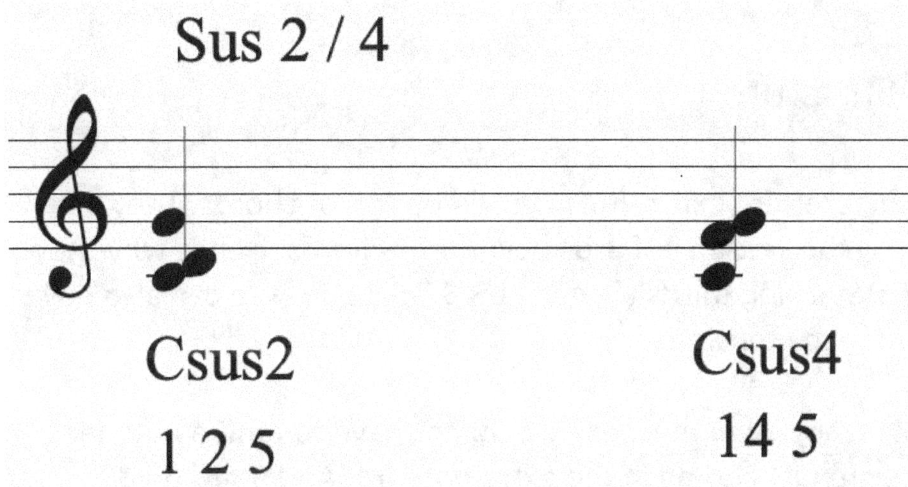

Sus is short for suspended. Suspended chords are created when we raise or lower
the third by one scale degree. Lowering the third to the second is Sus 2 and
raising the third to the fourth is Sus 4.

So, E moves to D for sus 2 and E moves to F for sus 4. Instead of 135 we get 125 or
145. You can do this with any type of triad or 7th chord, but you must make sure
they do not have a 3rd anywhere in the chord, or else it is not a true sus chord.

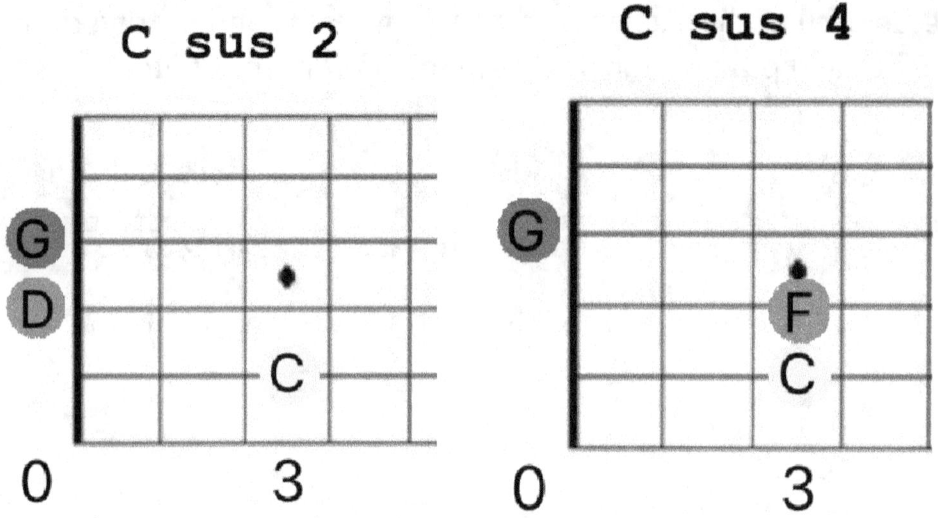

Tensions/Upper Structure

Tensions or upper structures are extensions we add on top of chords. They are derived from continuing the stacking of 3rds beyond 7th chords. Hence why they are called 9, 11 and 13. Stacking thirds we get: 1 3 5 7 9 11 13. We can also have flat or sharp versions of each tension.

This is different from a suspension, because we do not have to omit a note in place of a tension. We are just adding in the extra note. Ex. Add 9 or Add 13

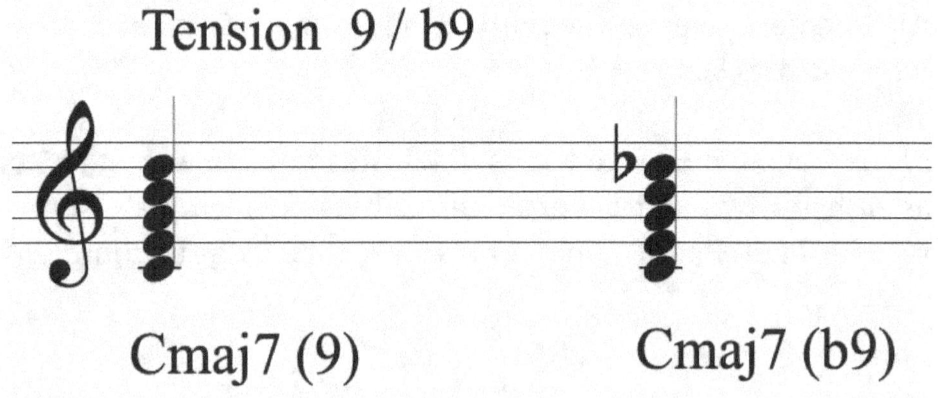

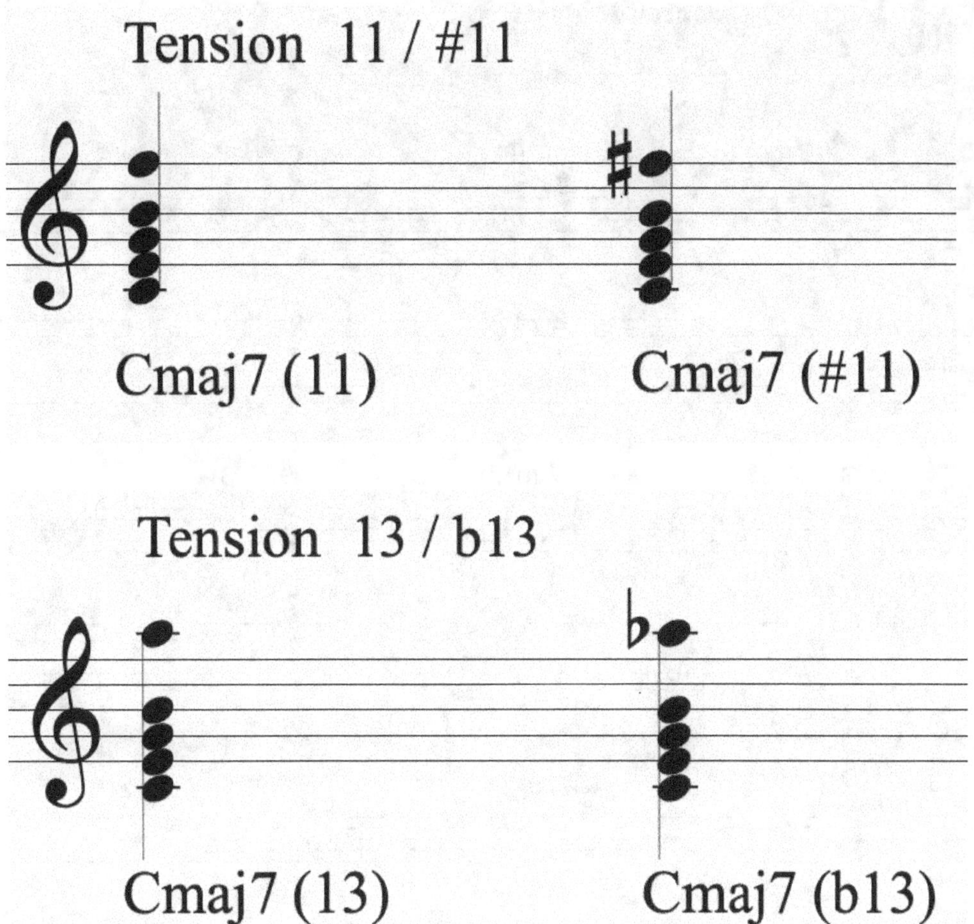

Many of the tensions/upper structures are determined by the scale or key you are in, but you as a composer or improviser can do whatever you think sounds good with them. Even if the note you add is not in your scale or key. Ex. Cmaj7 (#11) is not in the key of C, but it may sound great to add it into your music anyway.

When changing your chord shapes, it is helpful to remember 9 is above the root, 11 is above the third and 13 is above the fifth. You can easily raise each of these notes to add in the tension in place of each note.

Of course, you can also lower third to 9, lower fifth to 11 or lower seventh to 13.

Adding Tensions to Chord Shapes

adding b9, 9, #9, 11, #11, b13, 13

Jared E. Davis

Cmaj7

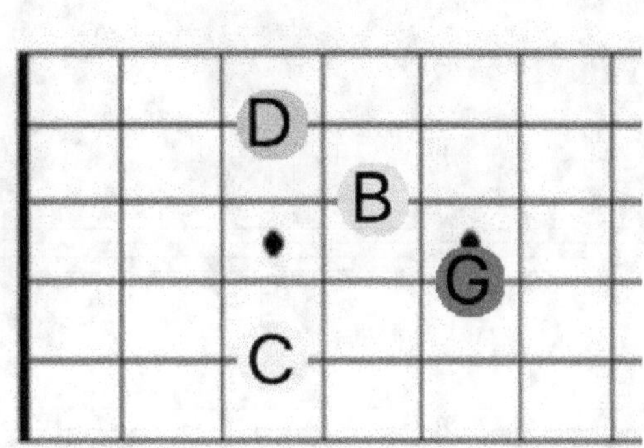

Cmaj7 (13)

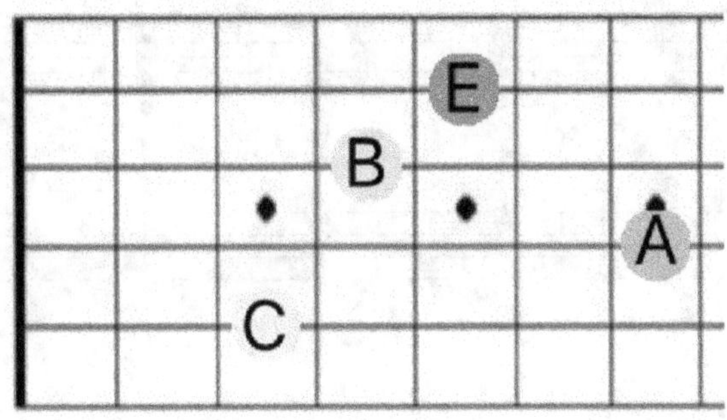

D is the 9 and A is the 13.

Chord Progressions

Chord progressions are a sequence of chords. For example, I might write a song and have a chord progression of Amin7 Dmin7 G7 Cmaj7. These are all chords in the key of C and have the roman numerals vi ii V I.

There are lots of different chord progressions, but some are extremely common.

I - IV - V   I - vi - IV - V   I - vi – ii – V   iii – vi – ii – V - I

This is how the "Nashville Numbers" work. It is just a way for us to be able to play chord progression and easily move to other keys.

Movable Progressions
"Nashville Numbers"
Jared E. Davis

Playing over chords in a Key

Pentatonic for each chord in key of A

Jared E. Davis

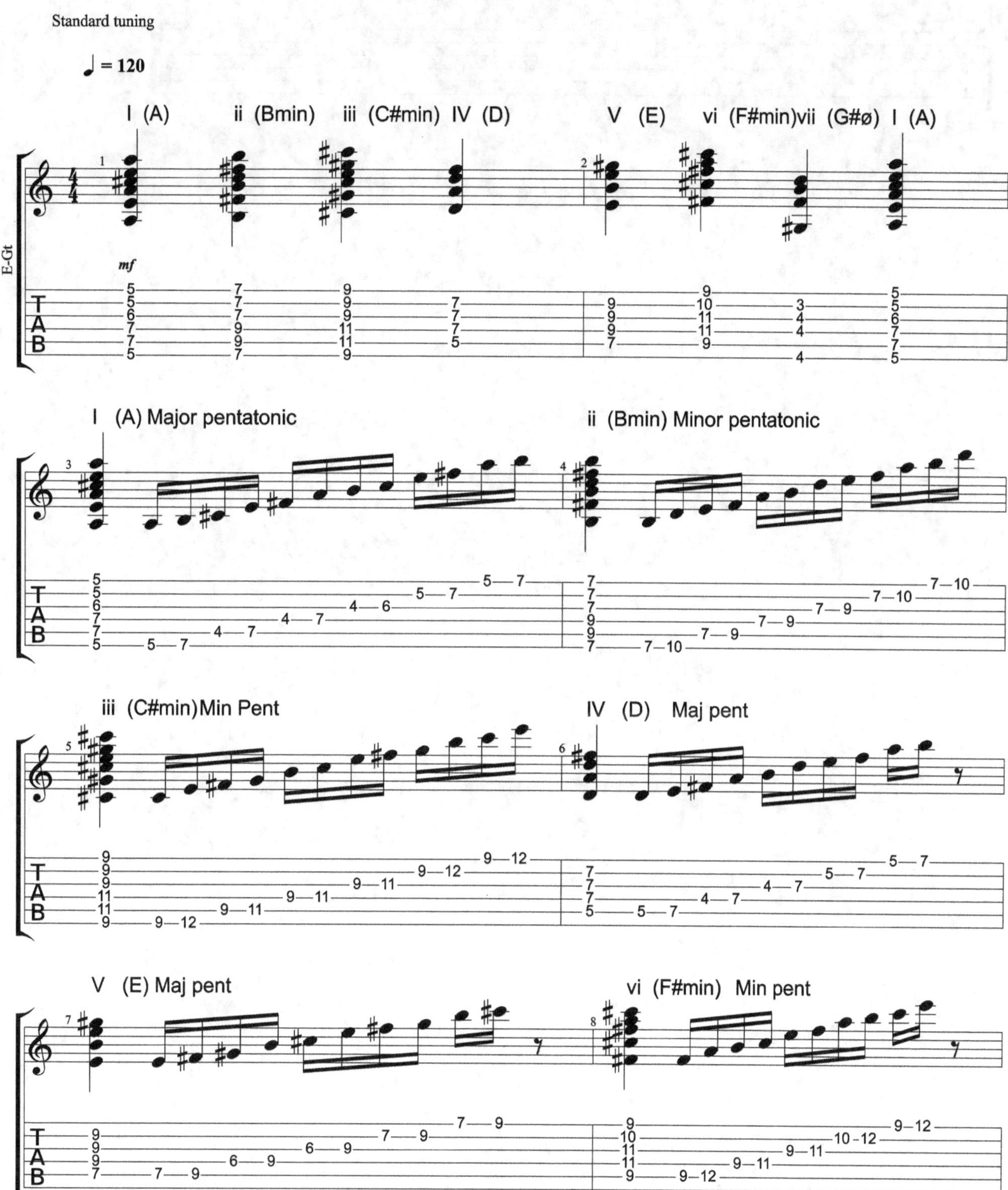

vii (G#ø) Min flat 5 pent

If I say the chords to our song are C – F – G. You will only be able to play those 3 chords. Whereas, if I say its I – IV – V, you can use that info to play in any key.

This became popular in Nashville because they work with lots of singers, and every singer has a different range of keys they can comfortably sing in. So, every time you get a new singer, you may have to change keys even if you record the same song for each singer. Practice these progressions in a few different keys.

Analyze Tunes

You should practice analyzing the chord changes of as many songs that you can. This is identifying what key the song is in and what are the roman numerals. Not every tune fits perfectly into a key. It may have multiple keys or none, but 90% of music on the radio can easily be analyzed with roman numerals. Tip: if you see two Maj chords a whole-step apart, they're most likely the IV V.

Diatonic 7th Chords in Modes

You can also take a mode as its own scale and create chords from stacked thirds like we do with the major scale. The chords from modes give us many new roman numerals not found in a major or minor key. All of which you can use in your music. This is called mode mixture or modal interchange.

It basically means you can borrow roman numeral chords from modes and insert them into your chord changes.

 Ex: instead of Imaj7 - IVmaj7 - V7, you can have Imaj7 - bVIImaj7 - V7.

The bVII7 is borrowed from the Mixolydian mode and is replacing the IVmaj7.

All of these roman numeral chords are fair game. Try them out and make up your own progressions.

You can also just use the triads by taking off the top note or 7th chord tone of each chord. This will turn them all into 3 note triads instead of 4 note 7th chords.

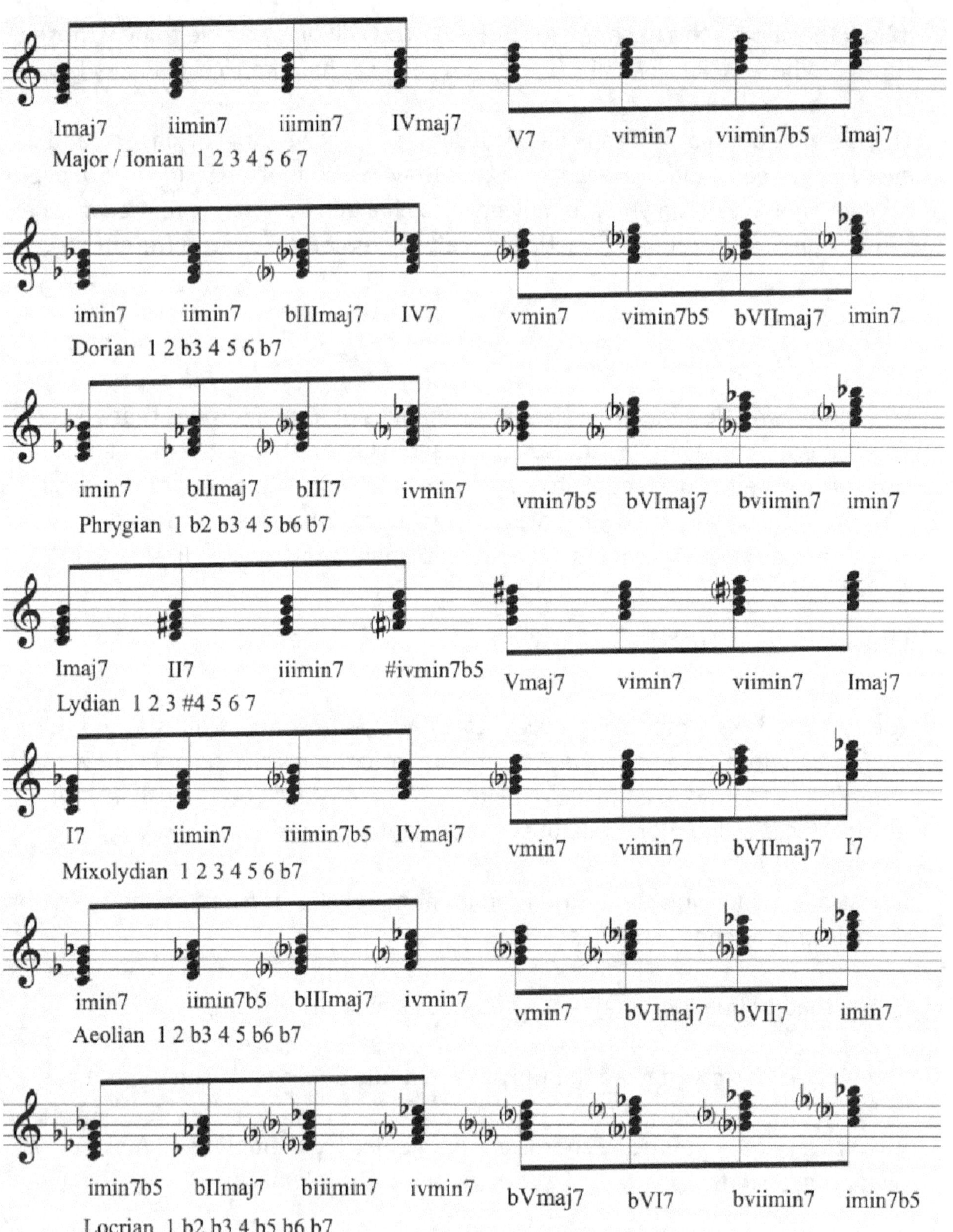

Imaj7   iimin7   iiimin7   IVmaj7   V7   vimin7   viimin7b5   Imaj7
Major / Ionian 1 2 3 4 5 6 7
imin7   iimin7   bIIImaj7   IV7   vmin7   vimin7b5   bVIImaj7   imin7
Dorian 1 2 b3 4 5 6 b7
imin7   bIImaj7   bIII7   ivmin7   vmin7b5   bVImaj7   bviimin7   imin7
Phrygian 1 b2 b3 4 5 b6 b7
Imaj7   II7   iiimin7   #ivmin7b5   Vmaj7   vimin7   viimin7   Imaj7
Lydian 1 2 3 #4 5 6 7
I7   iimin7   iiimin7b5   IVmaj7   vmin7   vimin7   bVIImaj7   I7
Mixolydian 1 2 3 4 5 6 b7
imin7   iimin7b5   bIIImaj7   ivmin7   vmin7   bVImaj7   bVII7   imin7
Aeolian 1 2 b3 4 5 b6 b7
imin7b5   bIImaj7   biiimin7   ivmin7   bVmaj7   bVI7   bviimin7   imin7b5
Locrian 1 b2 b3 4 b5 b6 b7

Arpeggios

Arpeggios are created by taking the notes of a chord and playing them separately rather than all together. The word Arpeggio comes from the Italian word for Harp. It basically means Harp-like. Take a look at this Cmaj7 chord vs. Arpeggio.

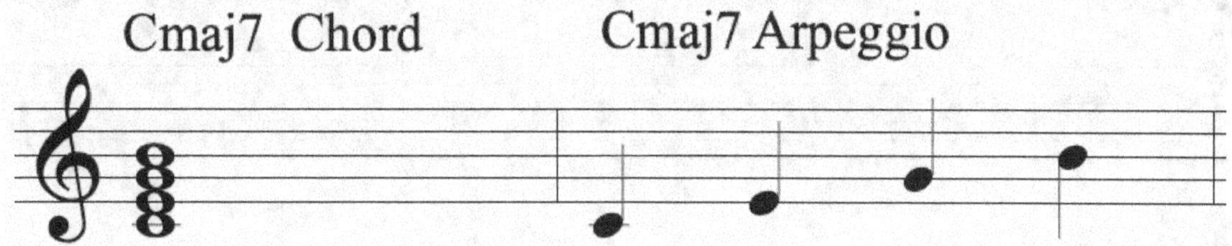

They both use the same notes C E G B, but the Arpeggio plays each note one at a time. Like a harp! You can make arpeggios with any type of chord and it is great practice to connect the chord shapes with the arpeggio shapes on the fretboard.

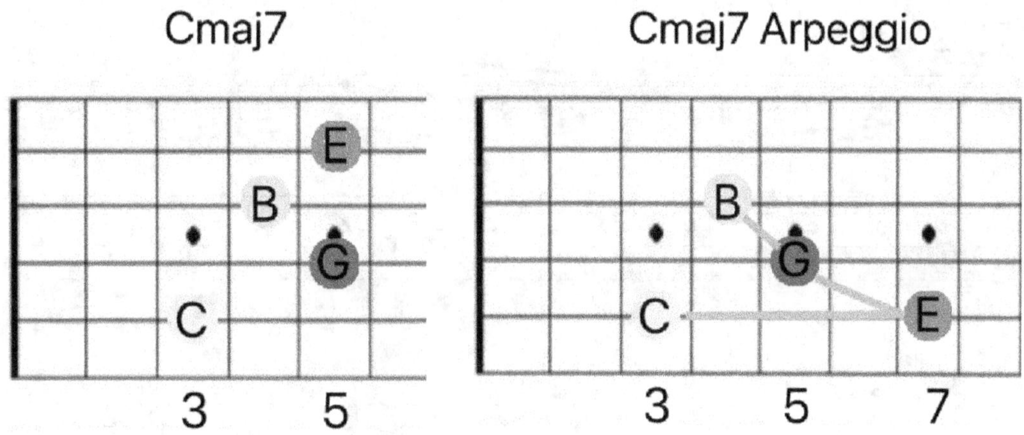

It is also extremely useful to think of the chord formulas when playing or learning arpeggios. For example, this Cmaj7 = C E G B = 1 3 5 7. Memorizing the arpeggio shape as 1 3 5 7 enables you to move it anywhere on the neck just like chords.

C major study - Pairing chords to modes/arpeggios

Diatonic 7th chords, arpeggios, modes in key of C

Jared E. Davis

Standard tuning

VI min 7 - A Aeolian
11
12
13
12
14
12
12 – 15
14
12 – 14 – 12
14
14
15 – 12
12 – 14 – 15
12 – 14 – 15
12 – 14 – 12
15 – 14 – 12
15 – 14 – 12

VII half diminished/min7 flat 5 - B Locrian
13
14
15
14
15
14
14 – 17
15
14 – 16 – 14
15
14
17 – 14
14 – 15 – 17
14 – 15 – 17
14 – 16 – 14
17 – 15 – 14
17 – 15 – 14

Matching Diatonic 7th chords with Mode / Arpeggio

Key of F - E String Root

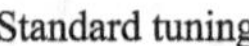

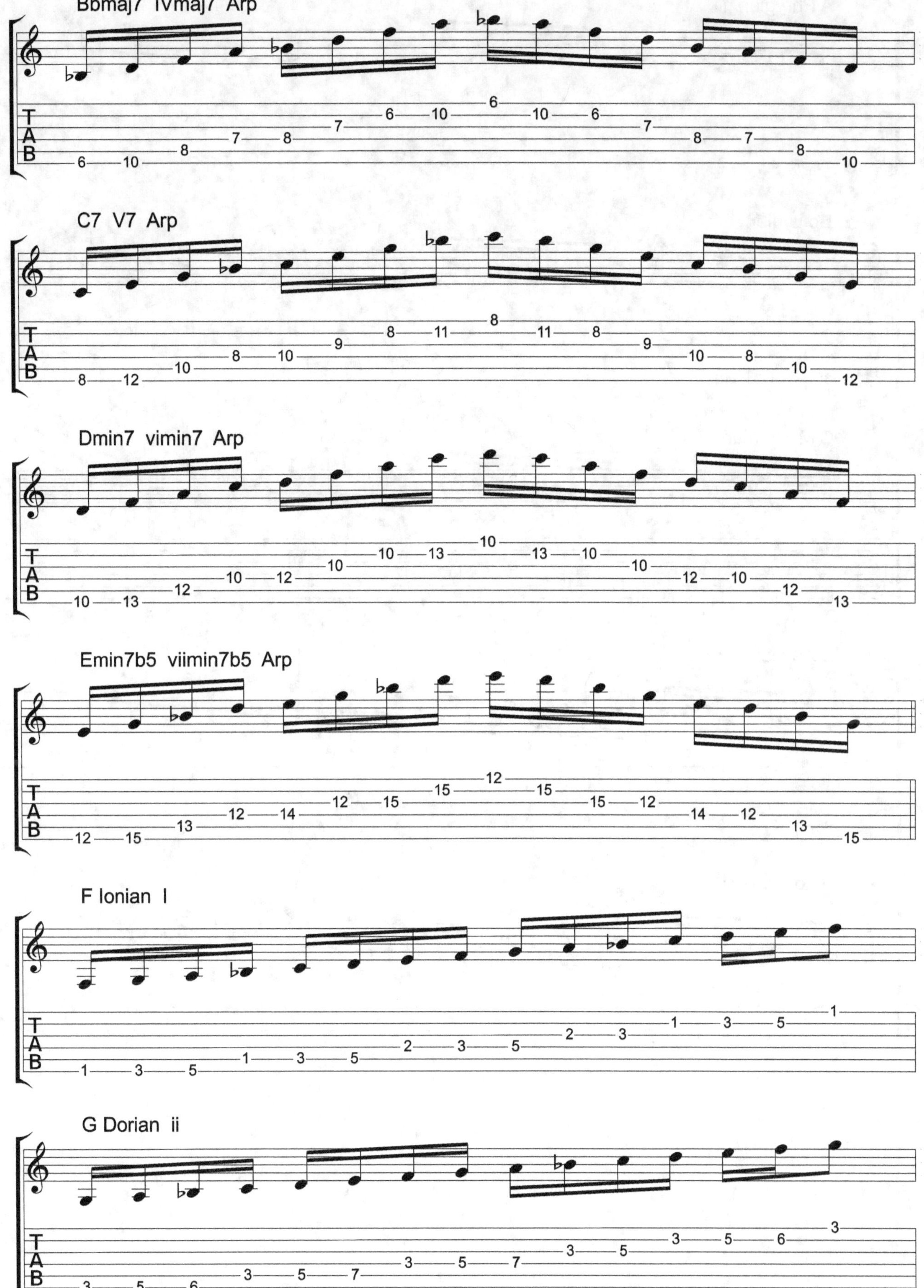

Bbmaj7 IVmaj7 Arp
C7 V7 Arp
Dmin7 vimin7 Arp
Emin7b5 viimin7b5 Arp
F Ionian I
G Dorian ii

A Phrygian iii

Bb Lydian IV

C Mixolydian V

D Aeolian vi

E Locrian vii

3/3

Pentatonic Inversions/Modes

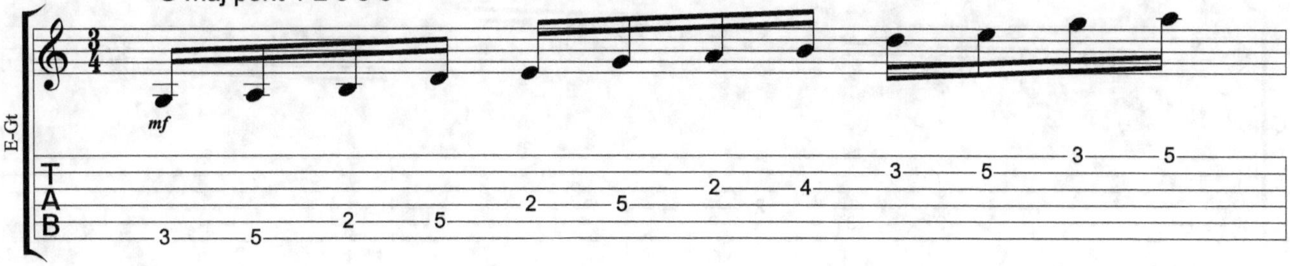

G major pentatonic / E minor pentatonic

Jared E. Davis

Standard tuning

G maj pent 1 2 3 5 6

2 3 5 6 1

3 5 6 1 2

5 6 1 2 3

6 1 2 3 5 or E min pent 1 b3 4 5 b7 - Emin pent is same as Gmaj pent. Relative maj/min, Emin is vi of G

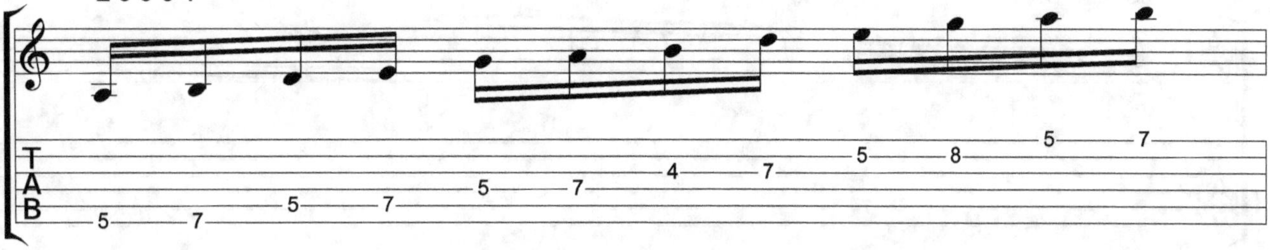

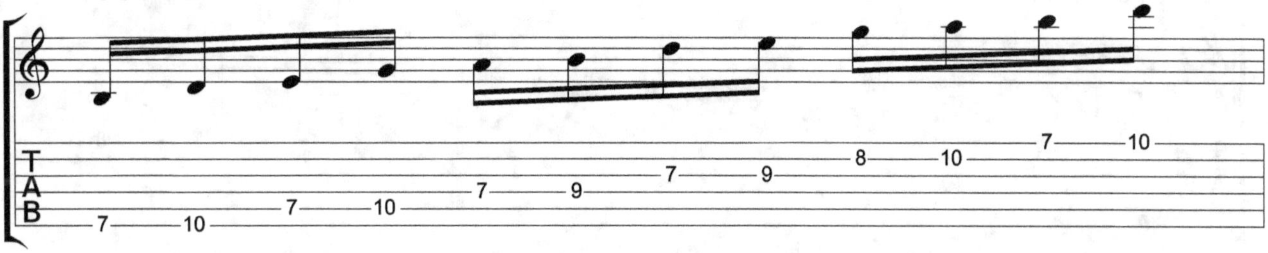

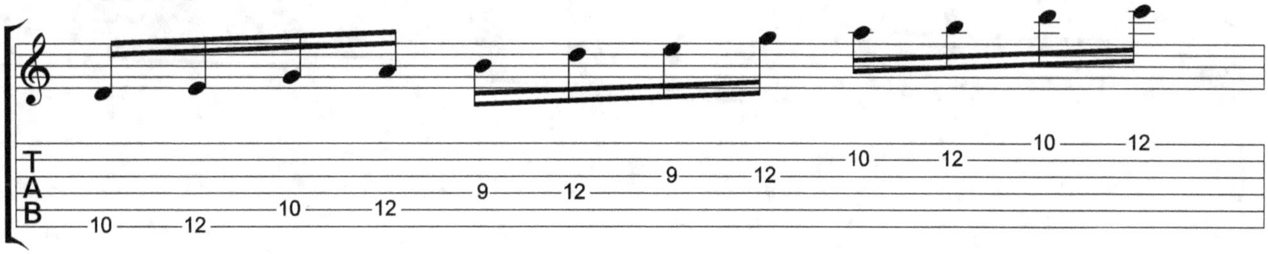

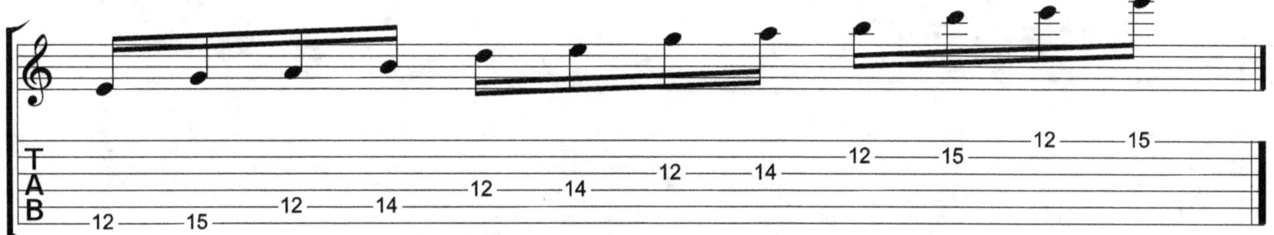

Diminished Pentatonic Inversions/Modes

F#min7b5 / F#half-diminished, vii° in key of G

Jared E. Davis

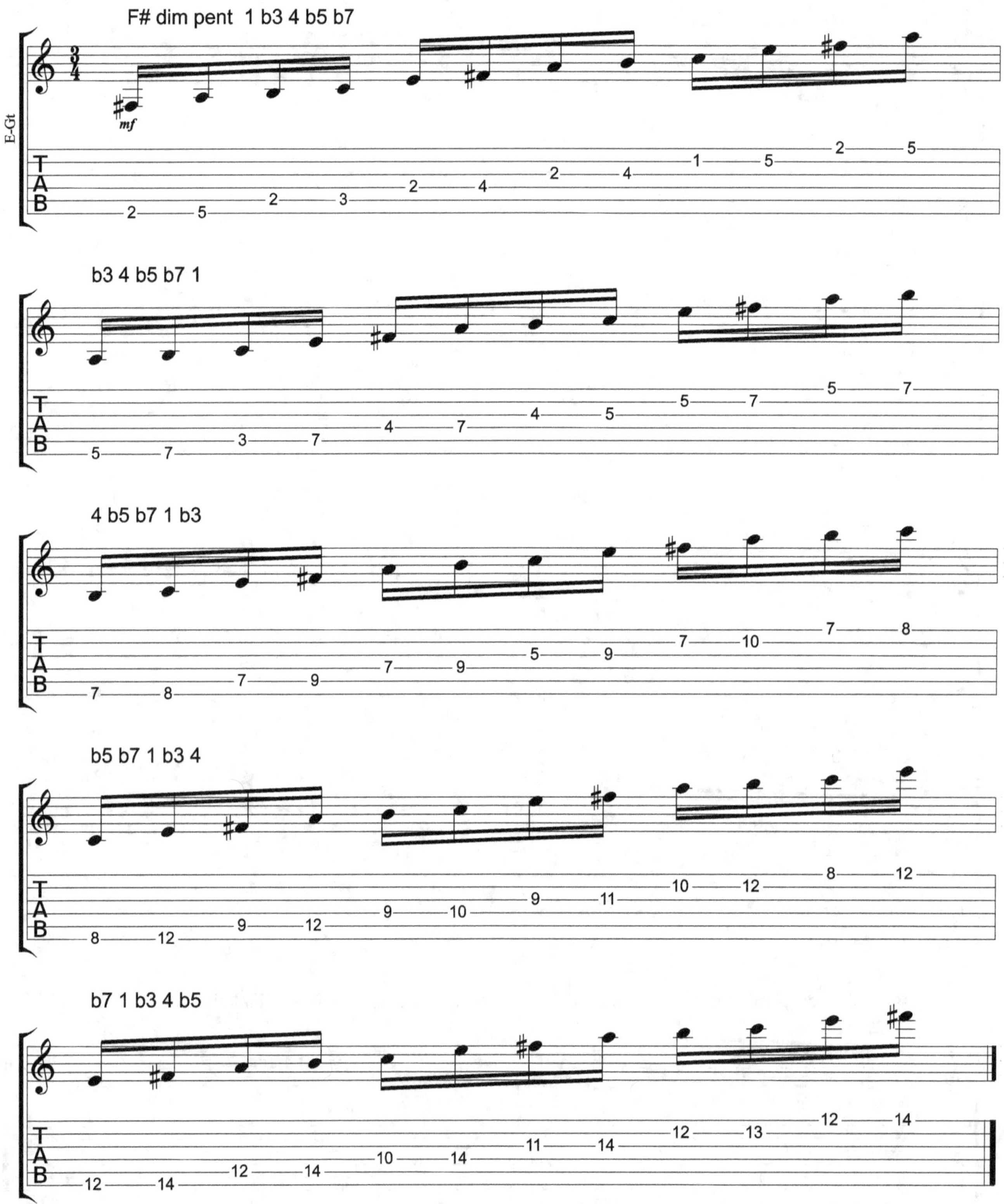

1/1

Inversions

Inversions are important to understand in regards to many concepts in music. First let's look how inversions work with triads and 7th chords.

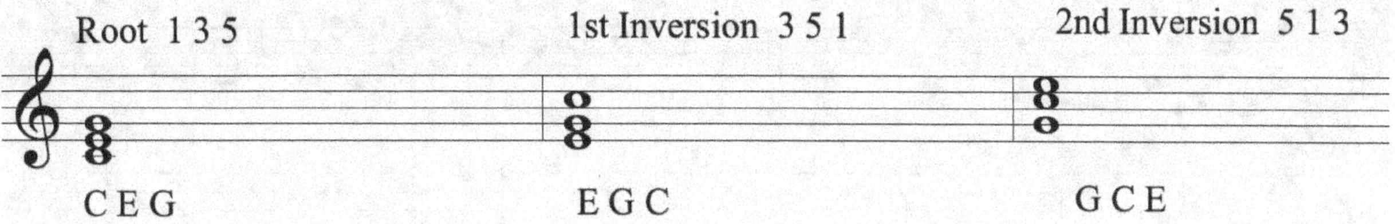

You can see in this visual that we keep the same notes, but change how we stack them. Root position is what we call the standard order, but if we raise 1 an octave it puts the 3 in the bass. This is called first inversion. Raising the 1 and 3 an octave puts the 5 in the bass. This is called second inversion.

No matter what inversion we use, it will always remain a C triad because we use the same notes, but inversions can give chords motion or a change in character.

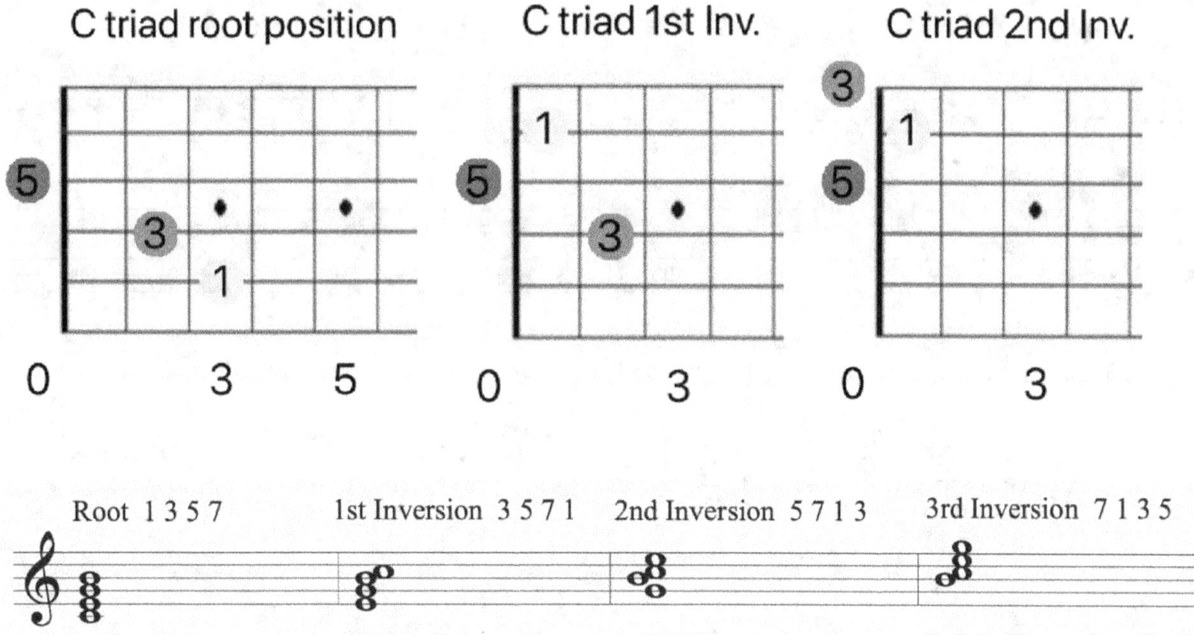

Same concept is applied to 7th chords, but we add an additional inversion to accommodate the extra note.

Triad Arpeggio Inversions
Maj Min Aug Dim
Jared E. Davis

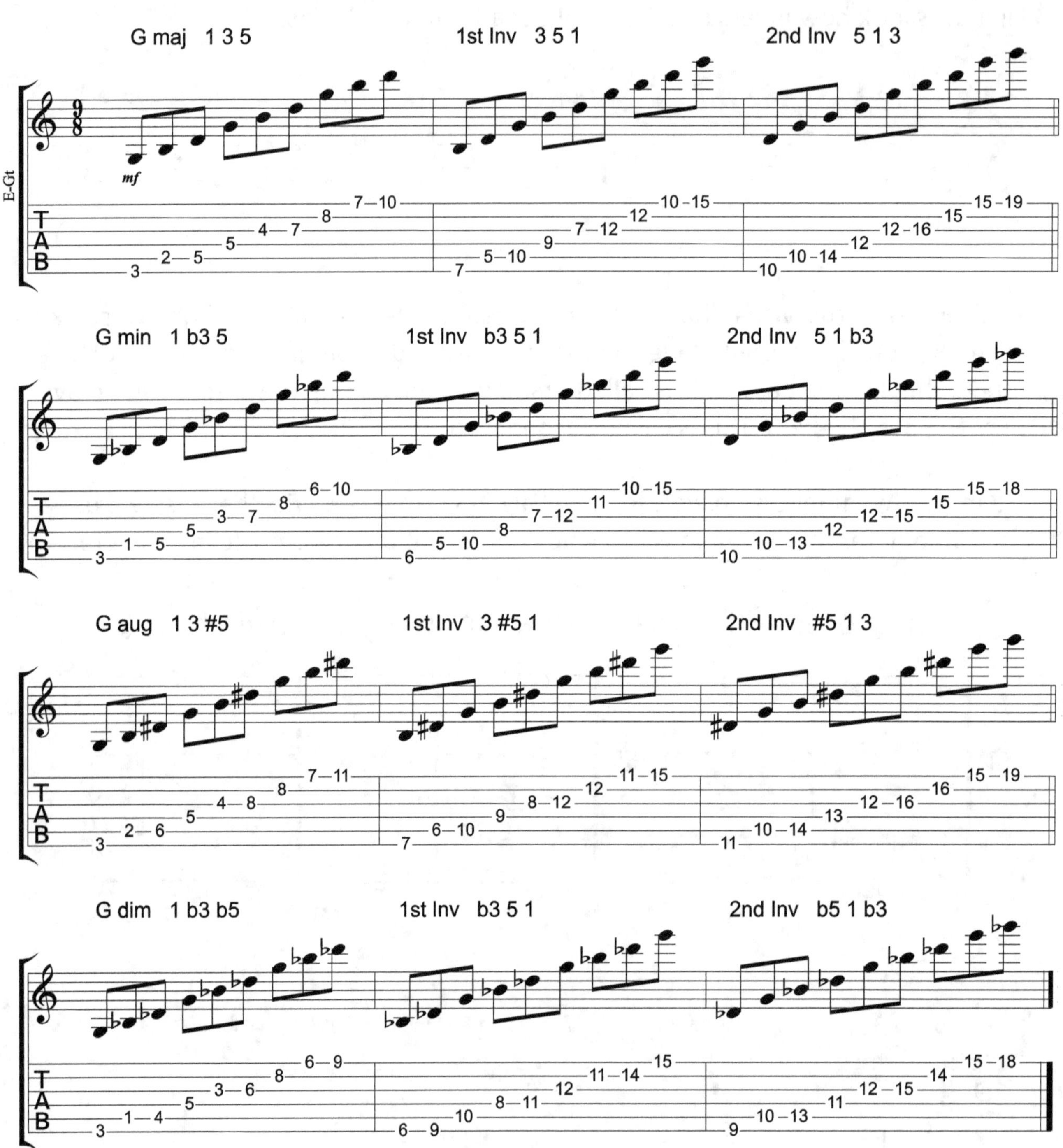

Movable Triad Arpeggio Shapes

Maj Min Aug Dim movable shapes

Jared E. Davis

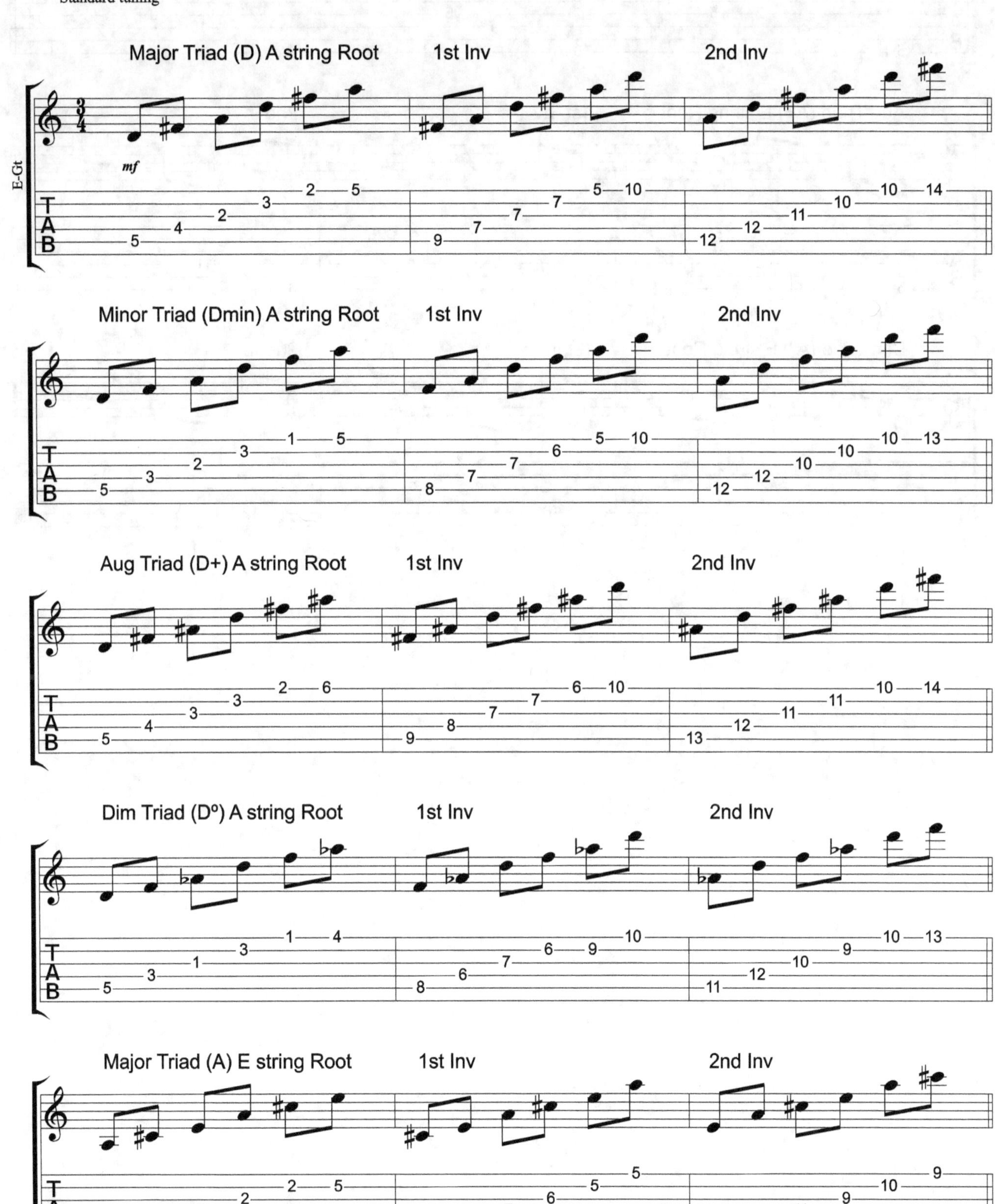

Min Triad (Amin) E string Root
1st Inv
2nd Inv
Aug Triad (A+) E string Root
1st Inv
2nd Inv
Dim Triad (A°) E string Root
1st Inv
2nd Inv

2/2

Root has 1 in bass, 1st inv. Has third in bass, 2nd inv. Has fifth in bass, and 3rd inv. Has seventh in bass.

These voicings are great for piano, but don't work well on guitar. These inversions are much easier to play and visualize with these types of voicings.

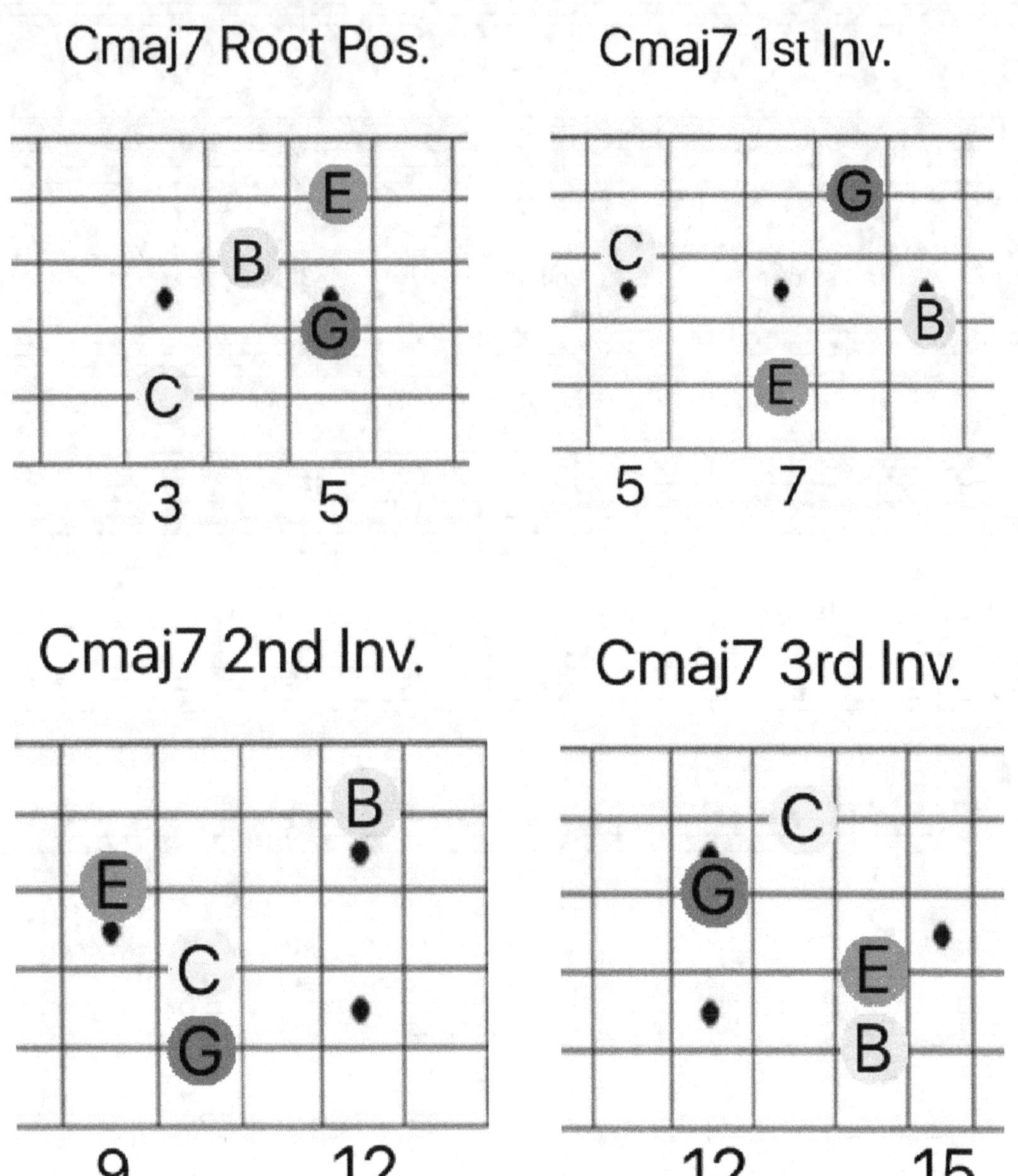

Basically, once you find a nice shape for a chord, you just move each note up like an arpeggio. Each string, no matter which one you look at, is playing the notes of the chord in ascending order.

7th Chord Inversions

Maj7 Dom7 Min7 Min7b5

Jared E. Davis

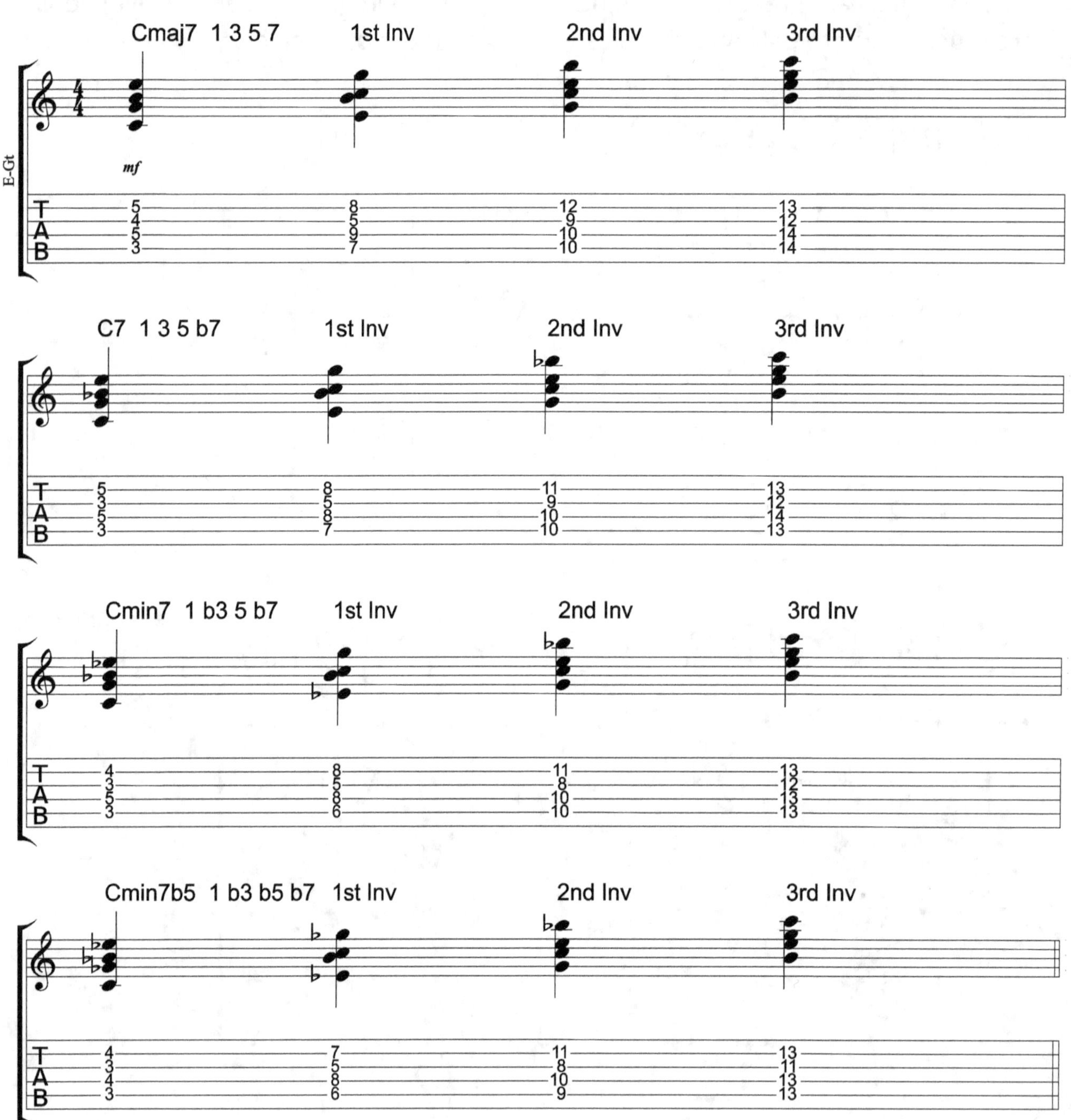

Gmaj7 1 3 5 7
1st Inv
2nd Inv
3rd Inv
G7 1 3 5 b7
1st Inv
2nd Inv
3rd Inv
Gmin7 1 b3 5 b7
1st Inv
2nd Inv
3rd Inv
Gmin7b5 1 b3 b5 b7
1st Inv
2nd Inv
3rd Inv
Gmaj7 Same as above, but move low E string notes to High E string on same fret

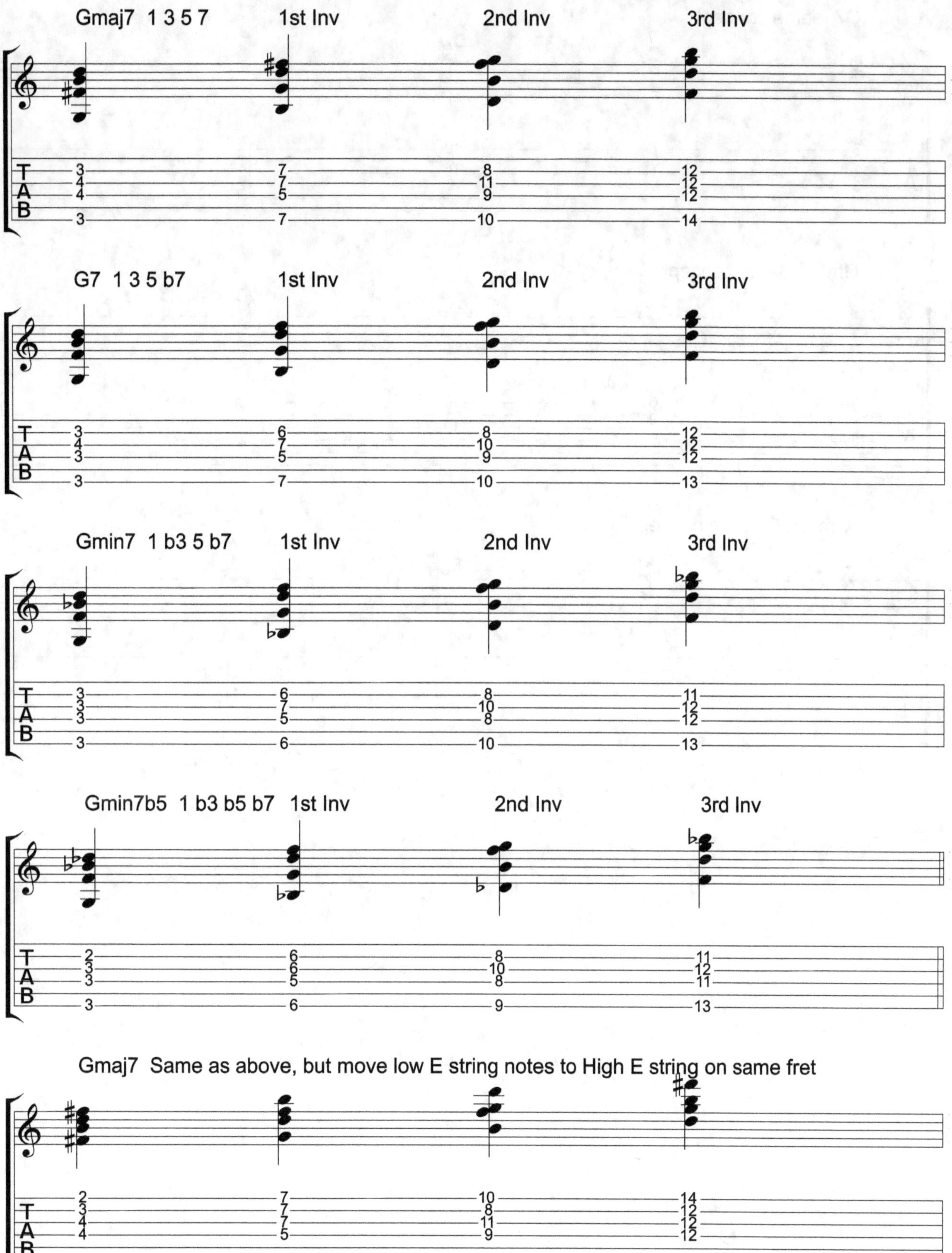

85

G7 same concept

Gmin7 same concept

Gmin7b5 same concept

Arpeggio Inversions

Speaking of arpeggios, these chord inversions work exactly the same for arpeggios. We just play the notes individually rather than as a chord.

Cmaj7 Arp. Root Pos

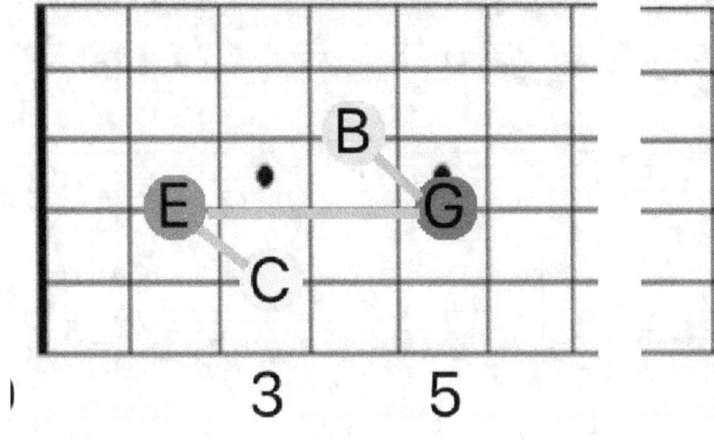

Cmaj7 Arp. 1st Inv.

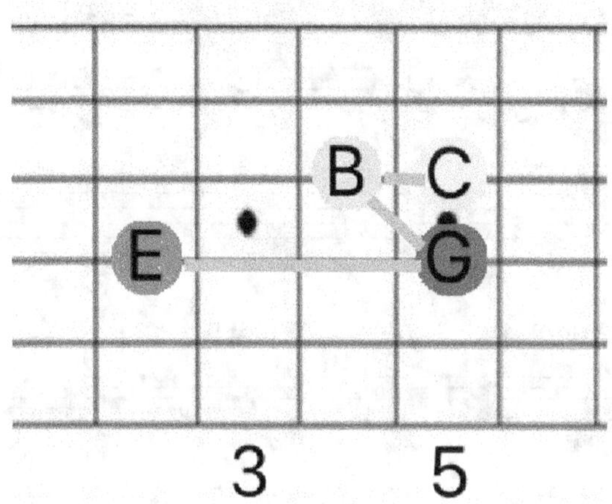

Cmaj7 Arp. 2nd Inv.

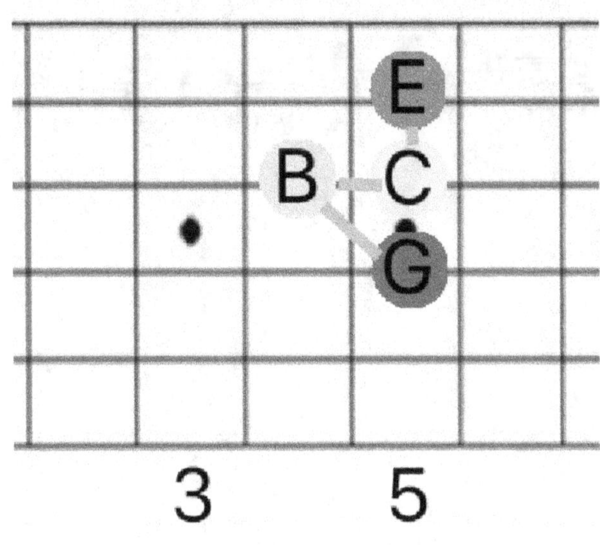

Cmaj7 Arp. 3rd Inv.

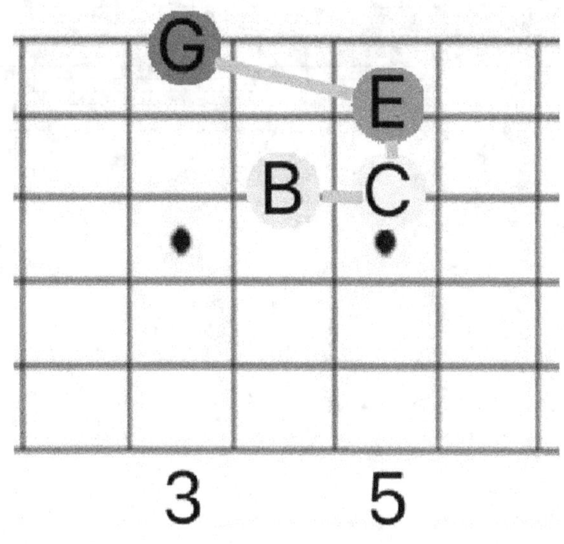

7th Arpeggio Inversions

Maj7 Dom7 Min7 Min7b5

Jared E. Davis

7th Arpeggio Inversions (Diagonal)

Maj7 Dom7 Min7 Min7b5 (half-dim)

Jared E. Davis

Standard tuning

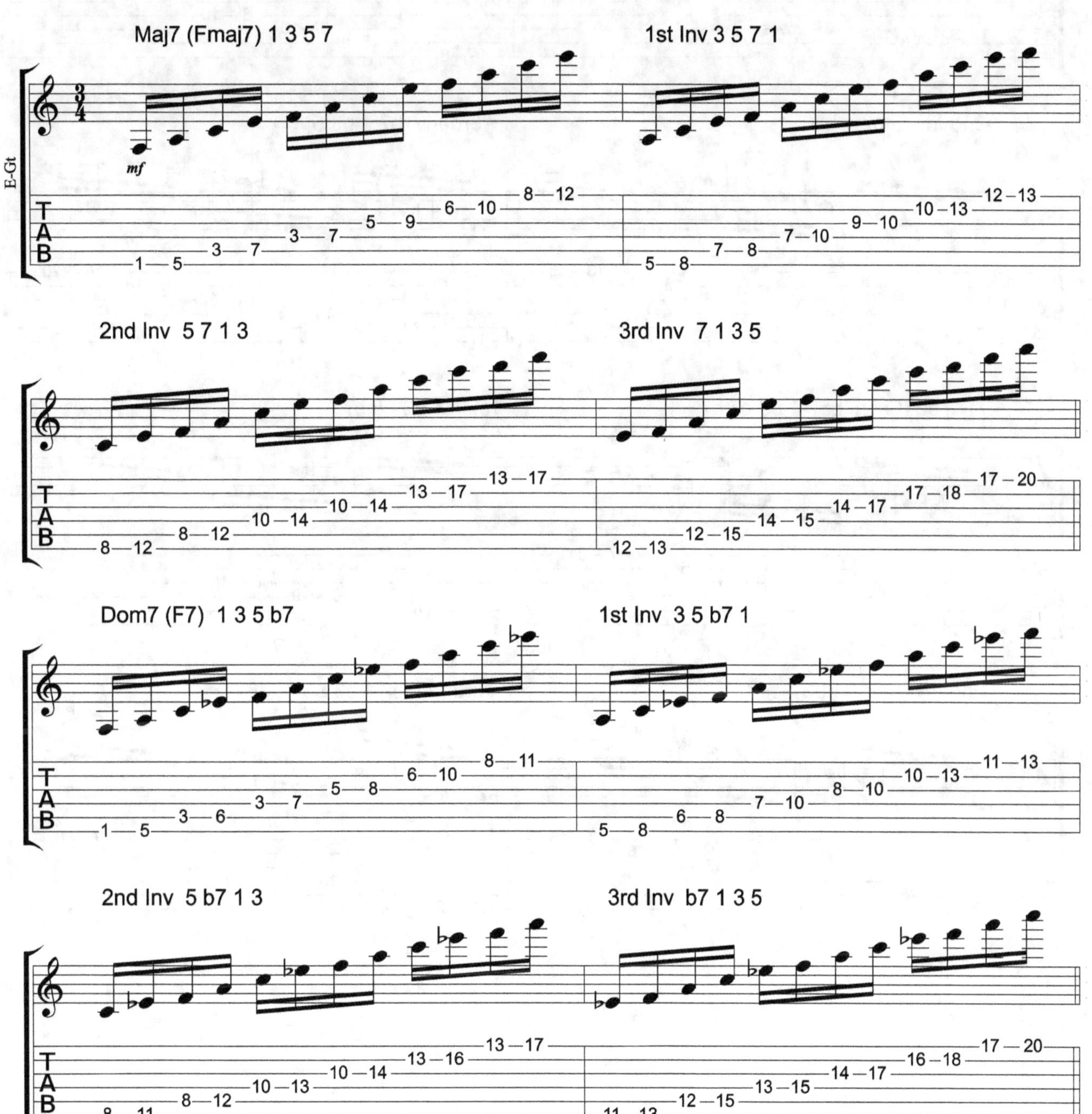

89

Min7 (Fmin7) 1 b3 5 b7
1st Inv b3 5 b7 1
2nd Inv 5 b7 1 b3
3rd Inv b7 1 b3 5
Min7b5 (Fmin7b5) 1 b3 b5 b7
1st Inv b3 b5 b7 1
2nd Inv b5 b7 1 b3
3rd Inv b7 1 b3 b5

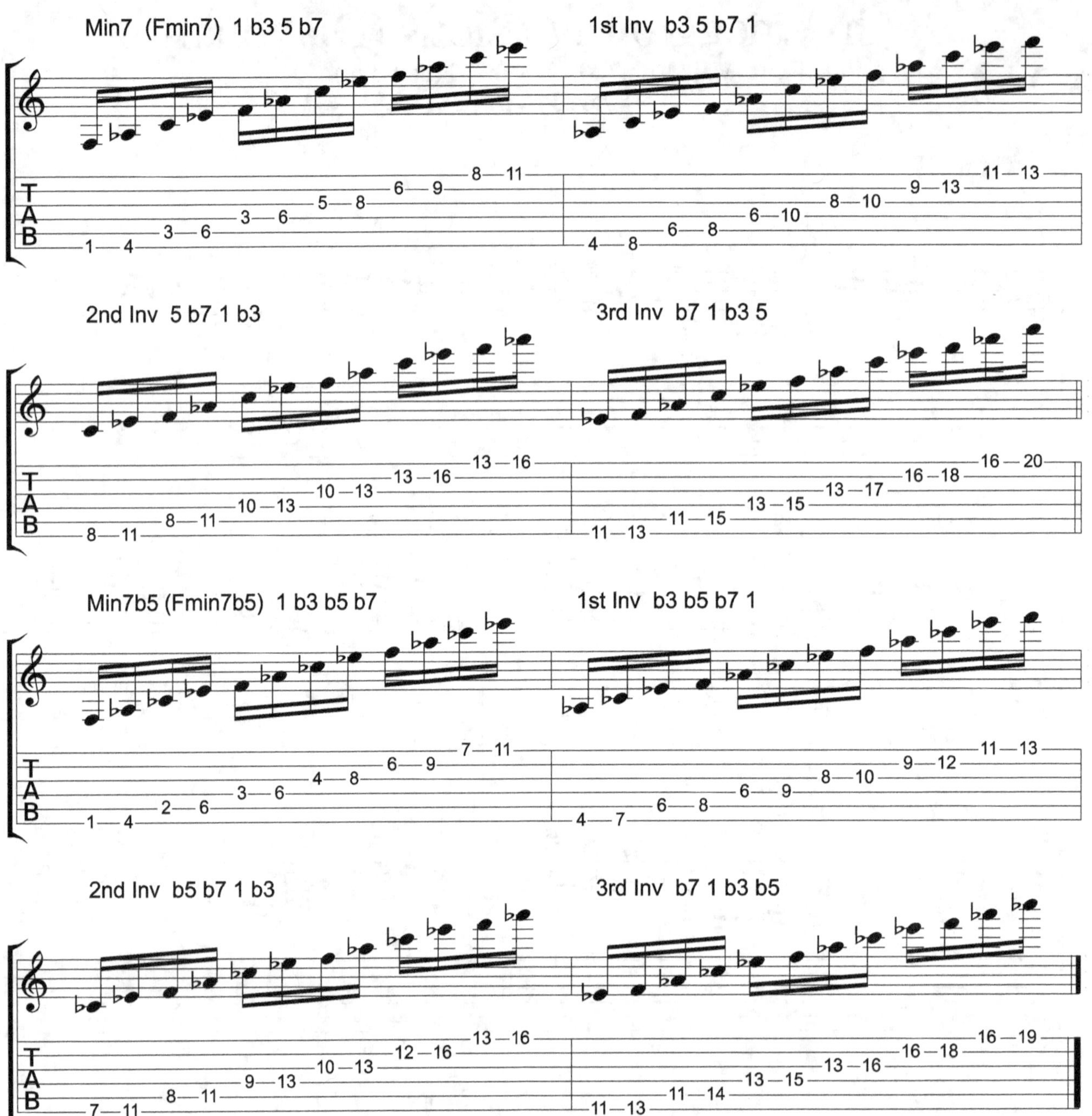

2/2

There are many different ways to play these arpeggios, but this should give you the understanding of how it works. Advanced players learn all the different ways to play inversions in different positions and string groups for all the chords and arpeggios. This includes triads, 7th chords, sus chords and chords with added tensions. Even pentatonic scales have inversions and modes are really just inversions of scales.

Diatonic Interval Inversions

Inversions also need to be understood with diatonic intervals and chromatic intervals. It is a little different of a concept when dealing with intervals, instead of having 1st and 2nd inversions, intervals invert to the opposite interval.

For example: In the key of C, if we have a diatonic third from C to E, but then raise C up an octave, the interval changes to a sixth.

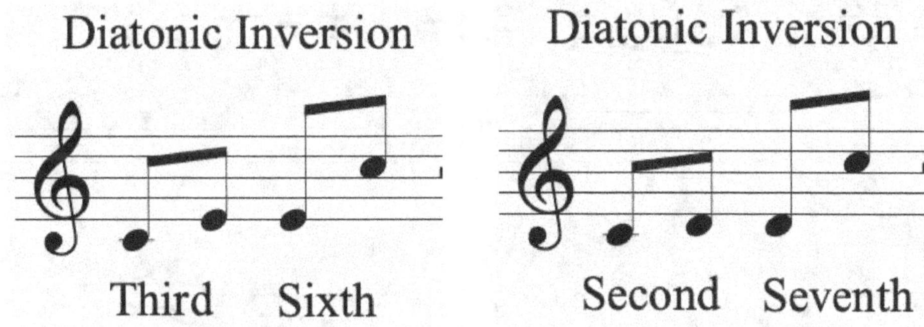

Or if you have a second from C to D, then take C up an octave, you get a seventh. Here is the list of Diatonic interval inversions. Inversions work both ways.

Seconds - Sevenths

Thirds - Sixths

Fourths - Fifths

Diatonic Intervals of Major Scale

Key of C 8th fret position

Jared E. Davis

Standard tuning

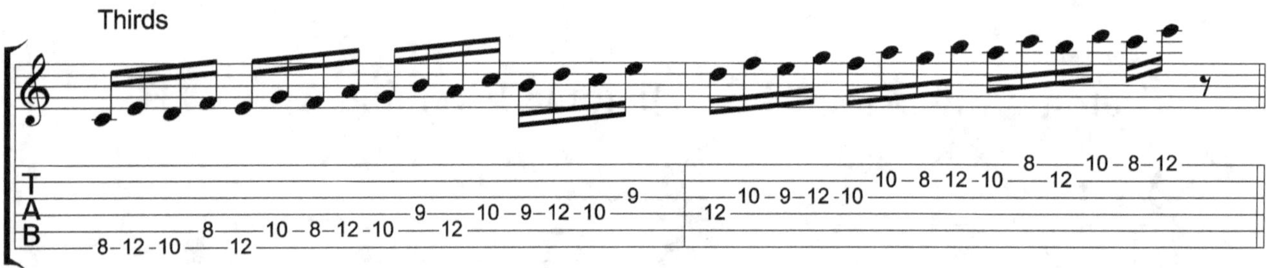

Sixths

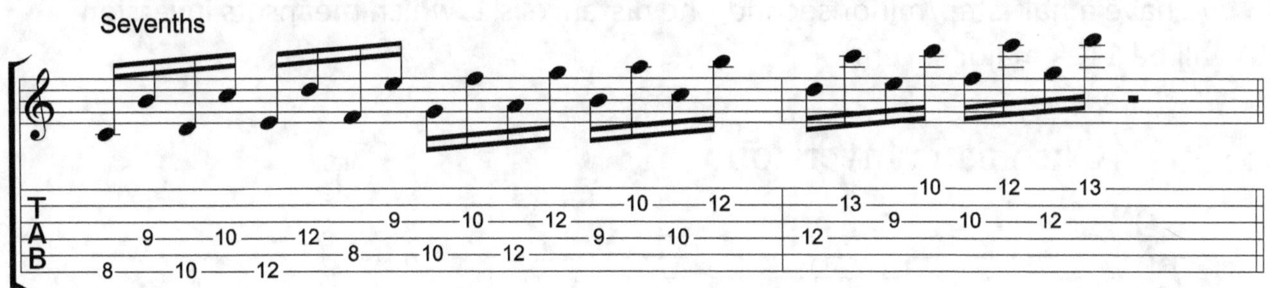
Sevenths

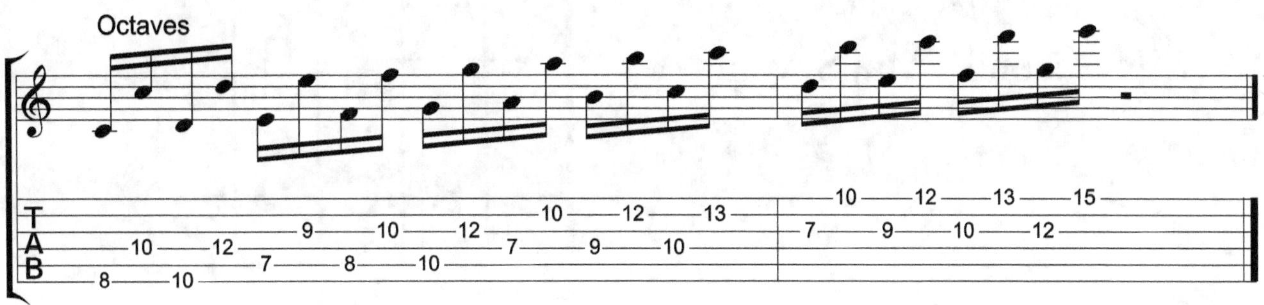
Octaves

Chromatic Interval Inversions

Chromatic intervals are a little more difficult, but the concept is the same. Each chromatic interval inverts to its opposite, but the opposite is more specific. Here is the trick, an interval and its inversion will always add up to 12. For example: If we have a half-step/minor second, the distance is 1, which means its inversion will be 11, a major seventh.

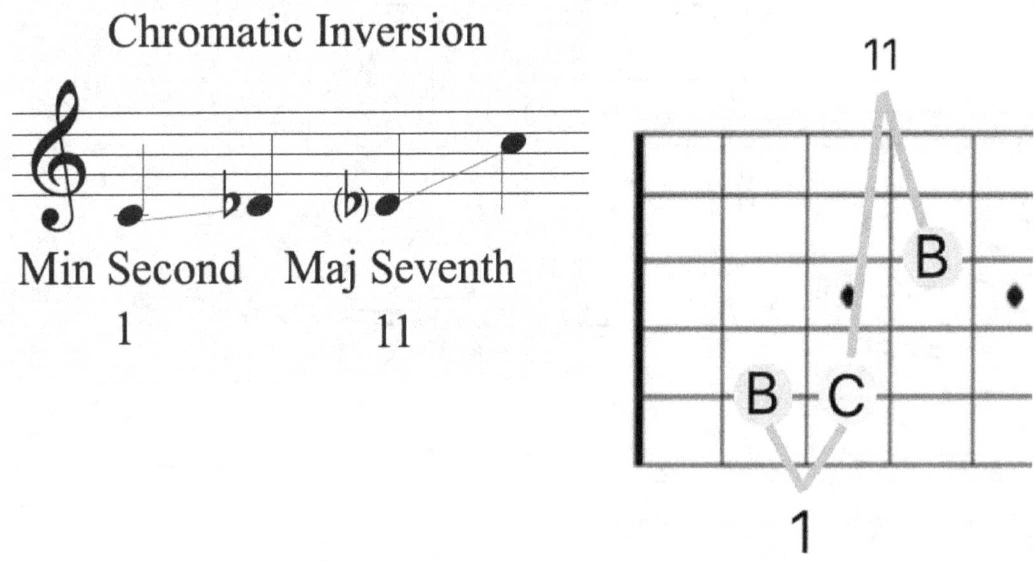

Here is the list of inversions for chromatic intervals. Inversions work both ways.

1 Minor Second - Major Seventh 11

2 Major Second - Minor Seventh 10

3 Minor Third - Major Sixth 9

4 Major Third - Minor Sixth 8

5 Perfect Fourth - Perfect Fifth 7

6 Tritone - Tritone 6

That's right, the tritone or b5/#4 inverts to itself. 6 inverts to 6. 6 + 6 = 12. I think that's pretty interesting. This happens because 6 divides the octave of 12 perfectly in half.

Minor Keys

I have been waiting to cover minor keys because they are more tricky than major keys. Generally speaking, minor keys use the same chords as major keys, but they start from the vi chord, or the Aeolian mode.

This means we use all 7 of the same chords, but turn the vi chord into the i. In the key of C, Amin is the vi or Aeolian mode 1 2 *b*3 4 5 *b*6 *b*7.

If we follow the A Aeolian scale pattern it will give us the same notes as C major. That's why we call them relative minor or relative major to each other, and that's why the circle of fifths lists the relative minors below the relative majors.

However, it doesn't stop there. Since classical composers really love the V7 chord, they decided to add it in to minor keys as well. This means that there are two types of V chords in minor keys. There is naturally a minor v and an artificial major V.

When the artificial major V is being used, it temporarily changes the Aeolian scale by one note. Raising the *b*7 to a natural 7 and creating a new scale called harmonic minor. 1 2 *b*3 4 5 *b*6 7

So, generally speaking minor keys are the Aeolian mode, but can also have a major V and temporarily change the scale to the Harmonic minor mode.

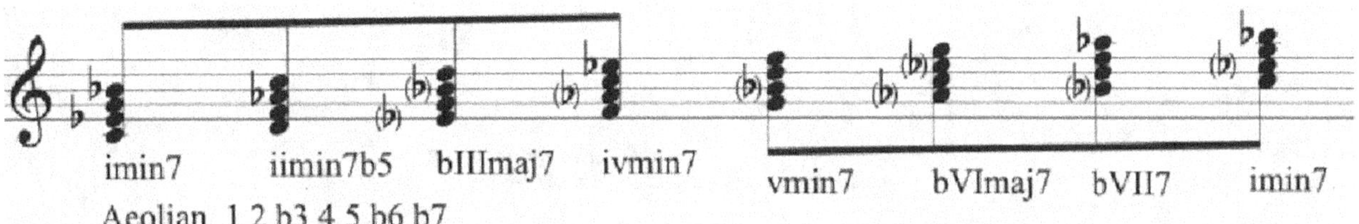

Minor Key Chords and Scales

Learning Minor key thoery of v and V, aeolian and harmonic minor

Jared E. Davis

These are the diatonic chords in C minor. Since we add an additional major V, there are 8 diatonic chords instead of 7 for minor keys. 8 chords and 2 scales.

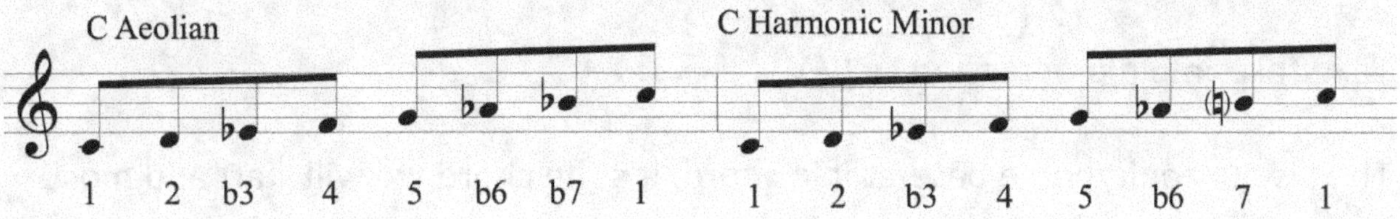

When composing or improvising over the major V chord in minor keys, you should play the Harmonic mode to make sure you hit the right notes.

Connecting Chords - Scales – Arpeggios

Now it's time to study how we can pair every chord with a scale and arpeggio. You can use easily visualize a whole key using the "Nashville Number System", which is exactly the same thing as Roman Numerals. Each chord in the key gets its own mode and arpeggio.

Luckily for us guitarists, we can easily visualize these chords on our fretboard. Keys are movable just like chords or scales. We just have to memorize what all 7 chords can look like as a whole movable unit.

When playing over any music, all you have to do is use this system to follow a progression. Simply visualize the progression on your fretboard and plug in the scales, pentatonic, modes and arpeggios.

Chord Functions in Keys

In the academic world, every chord in a key (including chords from modes) are assigned a function. A "function" has nothing to do with the type of chord or what roman numeral they are, but rather how the chords behave in a progression. There are 3 formal functions: Tonic, Sub/Pre-Dominant, Dominant.

Tonic chords are your home base and stable chords, Sub Dominant or Pre-Dominant (same thing) are chords with motion, and Dominant are chords with tension or a cadential feeling.

Take this simple progression I ii IV V.

The I is our tonic/home base/stable chord. It's the chord we will start and most likely end the music on.

The ii and IV are Sub/Pre-Dominant and create motion away from the tonic chord that leads to the Dominant.

V is the Dominant chord because it creates lots of tension and gives a feeling of wanting to return to the tonic chord I. We call a V-I movement a cadence. It sounds and feels like an ending. V pulls to I and I feels like home base.

These functions almost always behave in this cycle. Tonic – Sub/Pre Dom – Dom.

I prefer to think of these 3 functions as stable – movement – cadential. That way you can create any type of weird or non-tonal chord progression and still be able to apply these terms.

However, in academia they typically assign I vi iii as Tonic, ii IV as Sub-Dom, V vii as Dom. As I said, this is too limiting for my taste, but it's a good starting place to learn.

So, keeping that cycle of Ton – Sub-Dom – Dom, you can insert any of the correct functioning chords in that cycle to create a strong progression.

Tonic	Sub Dom	Dom
I	IV	V
Vi	ii	vii
iii	IV	V
vi	ii	vii
Etc…		

Movable Progressions

"Nashville Numbers"
Jared E. Davis

Secondary Dominant and II V

Secondary dominants are chords we can insert into a key that aren't normally there. Remember how the V is dominant and wants to resolve to I?

Well think of this concept as being movable to any chord. In other words, we can treat any chord as the "I" and give it its own V chord.
Ex: in the key of C E min is the iii chord, if we pretend E min is the I, its V would be a B major chord. Since B is a perfect 5th above E.

The chord B major (B D# F#) is not in the key of C, but we can use it as a secondary dominant that takes us to the iii or E min chord.

Secondary dominants can be a major triad or a dominant 7th chord. V or V7.

The chord symbol would look like V/iii or V7/iii. You can do this with any of the 7 diatonic chords.

Secondary ii V is the same concept, but we also use a secondary ii before the secondary V. Again, you can do this with all 7 diatonic chords.

Ex: F is IV in the key of C. Let's add the secondary ii V before it. C is the V of F, and G min is the ii of F. So, ii V/F would be G min - C going to F. ii can be iimin7 and V can be V7 as well. (G min7 – C7 – F)

A progression could look like, vi - ii V/ii - ii - V7/V - V – I

You can also use the minor version of a ii V. In a minor key the ii is iimin7b5 or iiø.

The V is still major or dom 7, but the tensions or extensions will be different.

Major V7 has natural 9 11 13 and minor key V7 has *b*9 #9 *b*13. & sometimes *b*5.

There is no *b*11 because lowering the P4 by half-step just creates a natural 3.

Secondary Dominants in a Key (open chords)

adding the "V" of each chord. V's must be major Triad or Dom7

Jared E. Davis

101

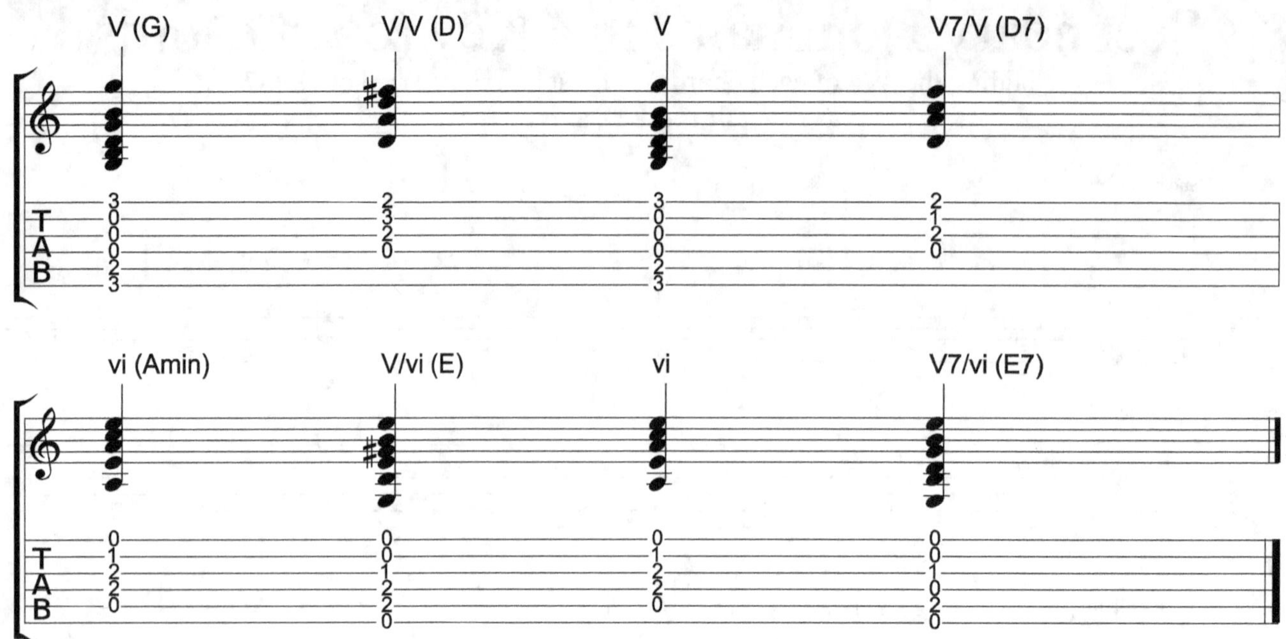

V (G)
V/V (D)
V
V7/V (D7)
vi (Amin)
V/vi (E)
vi
V7/vi (E7)

Secondary Dominants (movable shapes)

Key of C V/ii V/iii V/IV V/V V/vi

Jared E. Davis

103

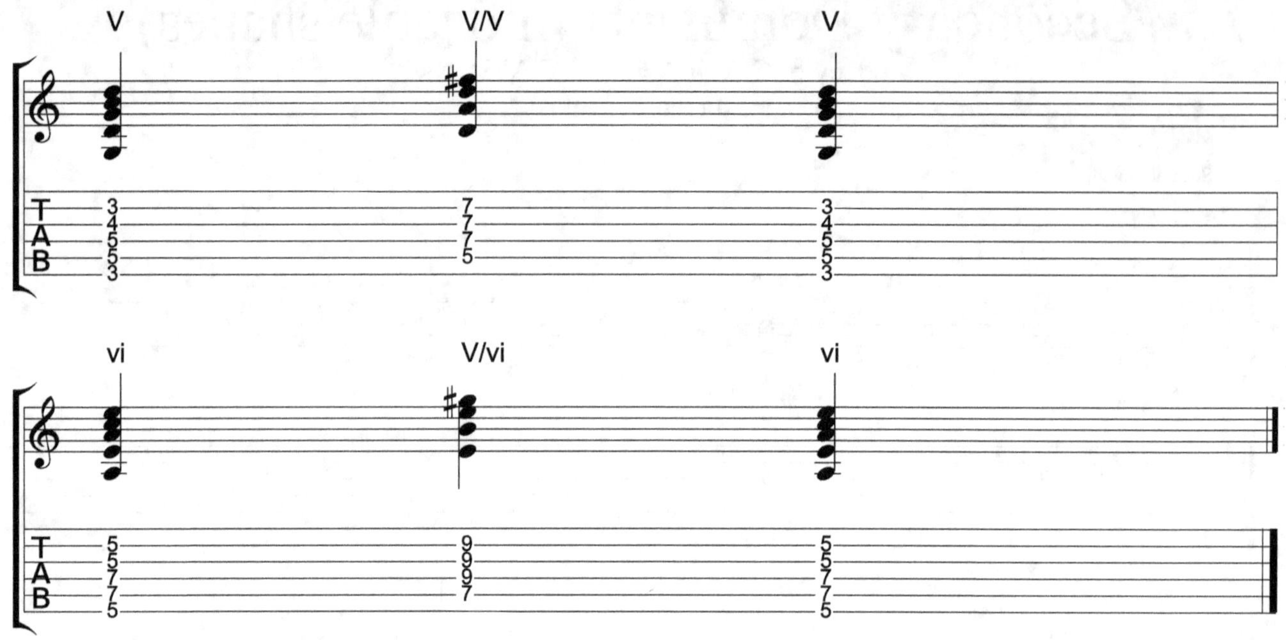

2/2

Voice Leading

Voice leading is a term that comes from choir music. Imagine the 4 notes of a 7th chord are 4 different "voices" you have to write melodies for. For singers, leaping intervals is much harder than stepwise motion. Therefore, when writing with "voices" in mind for each note, you want to move the notes from one chord to the next chord with as little movement as possible. Trying to keep common notes and using as many steps as possible rather than leaps. For example:

Bad Voice Leading

This example shows the movement from one chord to the next with no voice leading. The entire shape is just moving up a 5th. Each note leaps up by a 5th.

Good Voice Leading

In the example the voice leading is very good. We kept the notes G and B because they are also part of the G7 chord, and only moved the C and E notes by step. There are more "rules" than this, but this is generally the idea. On guitar we can't always voice lead perfectly, but we can definitely learn to move chords smoothly.

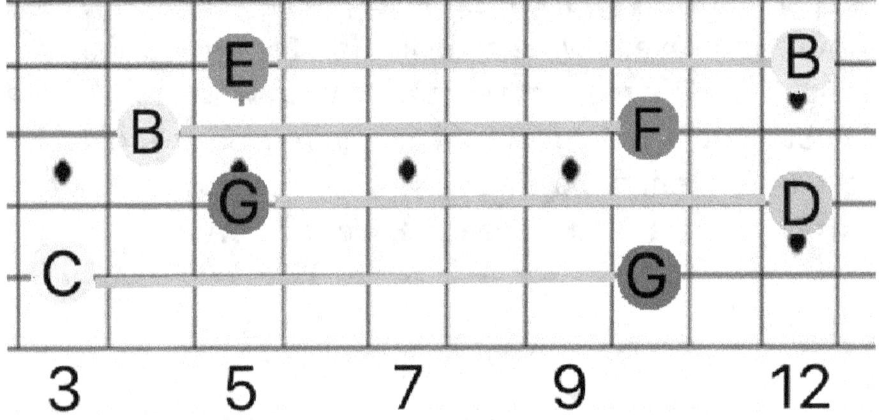

Each of these notes from Cmaj7 leap by a 5th to G7. This is how most guitarists play it, but this is an example of bad voice leading or no voice leading at all.

Good Voice Leading

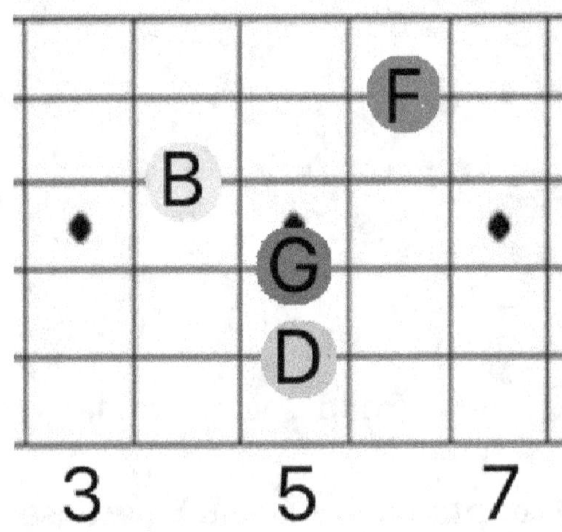

We kept G and B and moved C and E by step.

Moving the notes from the previous Cmaj7 to this G7 is great voice leading and learning to do this will set you apart from most guitarists.

Lines – Non-Chord Tones

Creating or improvising lines over chord changes is how we can create great sounding guitar solos or play over jazz changes. The basic idea is to create melodic lines that land on the chord tones of each chord as the go by.

Of course, if you only play chord tones, you will just end up playing arpeggios.

This is where the concept of "Passing Tones" can come in handy.

There are two types of passing tones. Diatonic passing tones and chromatic passing tones. Diatonic passing tones come from the key or scale, and chromatic passing tones do not.

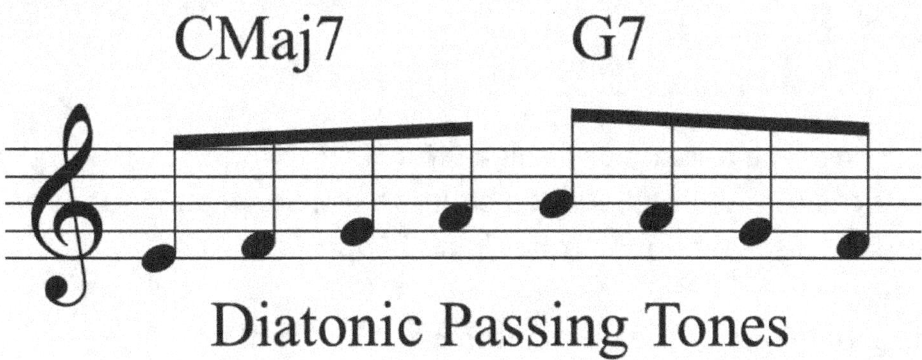

The notes F and A are the Diatonic Passing tones being used over Cmaj7. They do not belong to the chord, but are in between notes of the chord. Passing between the chord tones, hence the name passing tones, and only diatonic notes are used.

Same goes for the note A over the G7. It passes between the B and G chord tones.

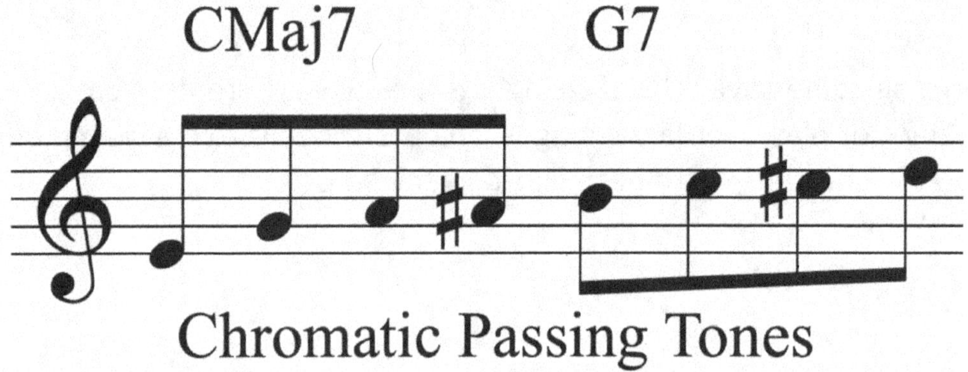

Here we have new passing tones A# and C# that do not come from the key or scale. Therefore, they are chromatic passing tones. Anywhere you have a whole-step, you can always put a chromatic passing tone in between there. This is how Be-Bop scales are made.

A is a diatonic passing tone followed by A# a chromatic passing tone. Which makes them double passing tones. You can have more than one passing tone in a row and can mix diatonic with chromatic passing tones as we did here.

Same goes for the C and C# over the G7. One diatonic and one chromatic side by side. They are double passing tones in between chord tones B and D.

Non-Chord Tones

Passing tones are just one type of what are called "Non-Chord Tones". NCTs are just the notes that dance around or in between chord tones. So, passing tones are in between, but there are also "Neighbor Tones" and "Approach Tones".

Just like passing tones, there are two types, diatonic and chromatic NCTs. Neighbor tones can be above or below the targeted chord tone.

In this example, E is the target note of Cmaj7 and B is the target note for G7. See how the neighbor tones are one note above or below?

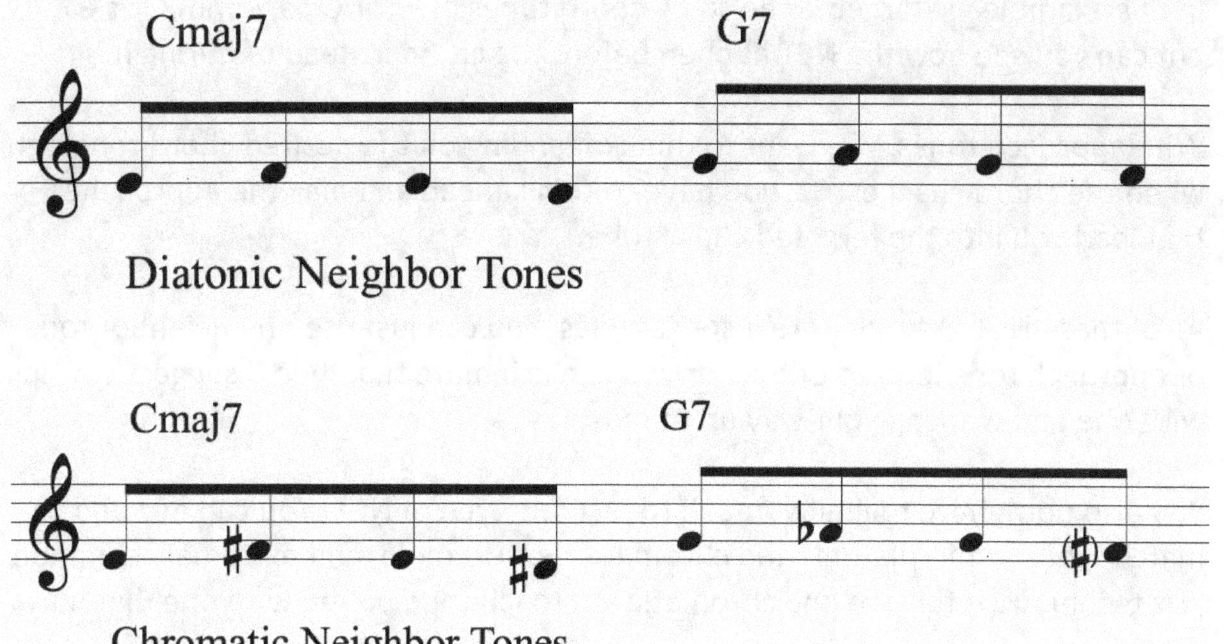

Diatonic Neighbor Tones

Chromatic Neighbor Tones

Approach Tones are similar to Neighbor tones, except they usually happen before the targeted chord tone and anticipate the chord change.

Diatonic Approach Tones

Chromatic Approach Tones

In this example we targeted the same chord tones of E for Cmaj7 and B for G7, but can you see how the NCT happen before the chord instead of during it?

With approach tones, you want to think of landing on the desired chord tone right when the chord changes. So, you have to think ahead and play the approaches that lead you into the targeted chord tone.

All of these NCT examples are just examples. You can just use one neighbor tone or approach tone instead of two, or you can use more than two. I suggest starting with one and working your way up to more.

You also don't have to limit yourself to just one type of NCT. You can mix and match types or mix diatonic and chromatic. For example, and extremely common jazz technique is to have one chromatic approach tone paired with one diatonic.

Chromatic below, Diatonic above Approach Tones

Studying lines is a long and tedious task. The best way to get better at playing lines over chord changes is to make "Etudes". An etude is like a little piece of music designed to practice a specific concept or musical idea.

So, pick a tune or song you want to learn to play over and write lines over its chord changes. You can map out the chords first and pick which chord tones you want to land on for each chord. Then just add your NCTs in and boom you got yourself an Etude! Don't forget to use your scales and pentatonics too!

You will learn to get more creative the more you do this. You will naturally start to experiment with using different intervals and different NCTs over time.

Here is an Etude, 8 notes per chord, over a typical chord progression of I-vi-ii-V

I vi IV V Etude

Playing lines over chord changes
Jared E. Davis

Conclusion

There is still a lot more to learn about theory, but I hope this lecture has helped you to understand the fretboard more clearly. Now you understand how to see the theory and figure most things out on your own.

As far as music in general goes, there are a few things I did not cover because they don't directly involve the fretboard. Such topics as Rhythm, Meter, Orchestration, Counterpoint, to name a few.

Although they do not involve the fretboard, I highly recommend you keep learning beyond this material. You now have the tools to make it happen and I am confident you will be inspired to do so!

Music is a lifelong journey and you can never stop learning. Thank you for trusting me to guide you this far and good luck!

If you need extra instruction or want to learn more with me, you can reach out to me about taking lessons.

Instagram: @jareddavismusic

Website: jareddavismusic.com

Email: jareddavismusic@gmail.com

Sincerely,

Jared E. Davis

About the author

Jared E. Davis is a composer, guitarist and teacher. His interests range from a deep respect for J.S. Bach, a passion for early atonality and a nostalgic love of classic rock. His current goal is to expand the palette of contemporary-classical music by integrating it with a multitude of other styles, such as rock, jazz, funk, and fusion. He also draws a wider audience to art music itself, through live new music performances at intimate venues.

 As a self-taught guitarist, he began performing at age 16 by forming his own band. After finishing his 4 years of service in the US Navy, he was accepted into Berklee College of Music in Boston, where he received his BM in Guitar Performance in 2019. While studying performance, he quickly realized his real passion was for composition and in 2021 received his MM in Music Composition from Texas State University.

www.ingramcontent.com/pod-product-compliance
Lightning Source LLC
Chambersburg PA
CBHW081345160726
48000CB00010B/3235